The Critical Idiom

General Editor: JOHN D. JUMP

34 *Biography*

In the same series

Biography/*Alan Shelston*

Methuen & Co Ltd

First published 1977
by Methuen & Co Ltd
11 New Fetter Lane London EC4P 4EE

© 1977 Alan Shelston

ISBN 416 83680 1 (Hardback)
ISBN 416 83690 9 (Paperback)

Distributed in the USA by
HARPER & ROW PUBLISHERS INC
BARNES & NOBLE IMPORT DIVISION

Contents

General Editor's Preface

The volumes composing the Critical Idiom deal with a wide variety of key terms in our critical vocabulary. The purpose of the series differs from that served by the standard glossaries of literary terms. Many terms are adequately defined for the needs of students by the brief entries in these glossaries, and such terms do not call for attention in the present series. But there are other terms which cannot be made familiar by means of compact definitions. Students need to grow accustomed to them through simple and straightforward but reasonably full discussions. The purpose of this series is to provide such discussions.

Many critics have borrowed methods and criteria from currently influential bodies of knowledge or belief that have developed without particular reference to literature. In our own century, some of them have drawn on art-history, psychology, or sociology. Others, strong in a comprehensive faith, have looked at literature from a Marxist or a Christian or some other sharply defined point of view. The result has been the importation into literary criticism of terms from the vocabularies of these sciences and creeds. Discussions of such bodies of knowledge and belief in their bearing upon literature and literary criticism form a natural extension of the initial aim of the Critical Idiom.

Because of their diversity of subject-matter, the studies in the series vary considerably in structure. But all the authors have tried to give as full illustrative quotation as possible, to make reference whenever appropriate to more than one literature, and to write in such a way as to guide readers towards the short bibliographies in which they have made suggestions for further reading.

John D. Jump

University of Manchester

Prefatory note

Where possible I have given page references to readily available editions of major works. Where these do not exist I have tried to give references of a kind which will enable the reader to trace the passages concerned with the minimum of inconvenience.

I would like to acknowledge the help given to me by the late Professor John D. Jump in the preparation of this volume: the interest which he showed went far beyond the call of a General Editor's duty.

A.J.S.

I
Some problems of the form

Writing, in his *Prefaces*, of the origin of one of his stories, Henry James makes what for him is the crucial distinction between the novelist – or 'dramatist' as he calls himself on this occasion – and the biographer:

> The subject of 'The Coxon Fund', published in 'The Yellow Book' in 1894, had long been with me, but was, beyond doubt, to have found its interest clinched by my perusal, shortly before that date, of Mr J. Dyke Campbell's admirable monograph on S. T. Coleridge. The wondrous figure of that genius had long haunted me, and circumstances into which I needn't here enter had within a few years contributed much to making it vivid. Yet it's none the less true that the Frank Saltram of 'The Coxon Fund' pretends to be of his great suggester no more than a dim reflection and above all a free arrangement. More interesting still than the man – for the dramatist at any rate – is the S. T. Coleridge *type*; so what I was to do was merely to recognise the type, to borrow it, to re-embody and freshly place it; an ideal under the law of which I could cultivate a free hand.
>
> (*The Art of the Novel*, ed. R. P. Blackmur, New York, rpt. 1962, pp. 229–30)

Here James, at the end of his career, reverts to that emphasis on the 'freedom' of the novelist which he insists on in all his theoretical writings: the biographer, by implication, is not free, but inhibited by the demands of accuracy and attention to detail which, paradoxically, militate against the achievement of a higher form of truth.

D. H. Lawrence, in his essay, 'Why the Novel Matters', makes a similar claim for his chosen literary form:

> And being a novelist, I consider myself superior to the saint, the scientist, the philosopher and the poet, who are all great masters of different bits of man alive, but never get the whole hog.
>
> The novel is the one bright book of life.
>
> (*Selected Literary Criticism*, ed. R. Beal, London, 1956, rept. 1961, p. 195)

The biographer is not included in Lawrence's list of those to whom he considers himself superior, but then biographers, while some of them might claim affinities with scientists, philosophers and poets, have rarely aspired to sainthood.

James and Lawrence wrote at a time when the novel might be said to have achieved its highest status as a literary form: it is perhaps understandable that they should have felt free to forget the historical context that might have reminded them that their earliest predecessors had often found it necessary to present their novels as pseudo-biographies. Their priorities, however, have remained by and large unchallenged, for in our study of literature we are, I suspect, still embarrassed by a form which is 'non-literary', if indeed we acknowledge it at all. Lytton Strachey, in his Preface to *Eminent Victorians*, complained that 'The art of biography seems to have fallen on evil times in England ... we have never had, like the French, a great biographical tradition' (Penguin edn., p. 10). Strachey's method of fulfilling that need was, in the fullest sense, partial, but his comment is a valid one. Compared with all the volumes of criticism that the established literary forms have attracted, biography has suffered virtual neglect. The list of genuinely critical studies of the form is short: the examination of individual examples has been the province of the literary historian rather than the literary critic.

And yet if literature has looked askance at biography, biography itself has continued to flourish. The attraction of an insight into not only the high points, but also the details of lived human lives – what Plutarch, in North's translation, referred to as 'men's natural disposition and manners' – can be evidenced by the statistics of publishers and librarians: the 'common reader' may not now be exactly what Johnson had in mind when he coined the phrase, but if his judgement is to be relied upon, the preferences of the novelist for a form in which he can create his own kind of truth can come to seem like special pleading.

The immediate attraction of biography for the reader is two-fold: it appeals to our curiosity about human personality, and it appeals to our interest in factual knowledge, in finding out 'what exactly happened'. The two aspects are, of course, scarcely separable, but they cover a wide and complicated moral spectrum. Mr Valiant-for-Truth and Peeping Tom are not as easy to distinguish as they might appear: to revert to another Jamesian instance one might ask in which of those roles we are asked to see the narrator in *The Aspern Papers*, that record both of the frustrations of the biographic researcher and of his devastating effect upon those with whom he is involved. Not all biography has praised famous men, and if awareness of the human instinct of curiosity has motivated a great deal of biographical writing our suspicion of that instinct can equally make us suspicious of the form itself. John Aubrey was fully aware of this issue, when he wrote, as his editor tells us, of his own *Brief Lives*, 'these arcana are not fit to lett flie abroad, till about thirty years hence ... for the author and the Persons (like Medlars) ought to be rotten first' (Aubrey's *Brief Lives*, ed. Oliver Lawson Dick, Penguin edn., pp. 161–2). It might be reasonably conjectured that as much biography has been written in response to the less noble aspects of human curiosity as in response to a desire for truth of scientific impeccability. One thinks, in this respect, of the range of reminiscential biography inspired by the Romantic poets, for example works like Edward Trelawny's *Records of Shelley, Byron and the Author*, with the unselfconscious give-away in the closing words of its title. Sir Harold Nicolson referred to Trelawny as 'a liar and a cad' and his most recent editor,

David Wright, points out delightfully that the reference to him in the index of Doris Langley Moore's magisterial biography of Byron begins: 'Trelawny, Edward John, lies and inaccuracies of.' None of this however reduces our pleasure in the memoir itself and Wright's own description of Trelawny as 'an imaginative manipulator of reality' could, as we shall see, apply to biographers with more respectable credentials.

There is ample evidence to suggest that even the most properly-motivated of biographers have always been aware of the stimulus of natural curiosity, whatever their stated purpose may have been. At a time when the Romantic emphasis on the importance of individual experience must have had a more than coincident relationship with a proliferation of biographies, memoirs and reminiscences, Coleridge saw fit to warn his contemporaries against indulging their baser motives.

> An inquisitiveness into the minutest circumstances and casual sayings of eminent contemporaries, is indeed quite natural; but so indeed are all our follies, and the more rational they are, the more caution should we exert in guarding against them,

he wrote *The Friend* in 1810, and whatever nobler motives biographers may have produced to justify their activities they tend to refer to the fascination of intimacy of detail about private lives with a regularity that might qualify the more moralistic elements of their self-justification. Thus Dryden, in his own *Life of Plutarch* prefixed to an edition of Plutarch's *Lives* published in 1683–6:

> ... there is withal a descent into minute circumstances and trivial passages of life, which are natural to this way of writing, and which the dignity of the other two (i.e. 'Commentaries or annals' and 'History properly so called') will not admit. There you are conducted only into the rooms of state; here you are led into the private lodgings of the hero: you see him in his undress, and are made familiar with his most private actions and conversations.

Dryden justifies this aspect of the form by its humanising effect: it cuts the hero down to size, 'as naked as ever nature made him ... (we) ... find the Demy-God a man', but the capacity to find a moral justification for the activity seems to have been instinctive in such cases. Johnson, one of the greatest of biography's practitioners as well as its greatest subject, expressed the belief that it could be a positive duty to examine the day-to-day activities of the biographical subject:

> ... the business of the biographer is often to pass slightly over those performances and incidents, which produce vulgar greatness, to lead the thoughts into domestic privacies, and display the minute details of daily life, where exterior appendages are cast aside, and men excel each other only by prudence and by virtue.
>
> (*The Rambler*, No. 60)

and it would be difficult to find a more accurate account of the methods of Boswell himself. Johnson, of course, can hardly be held responsible for the glut of 'minute details of daily life' that seem scarcely to have satisfied the curiosity of the later readers of his own century, or for the voracity of the twentieth-century academic biographer with his card-indexes, but his sense of the fascination of total immersion in the life of the subject has been echoed, if without its moralistic justification by, for example, Michael Holroyd in the preface to the revised edition of his massive biography of Lytton Strachey:

> My work held something of the excitement of an archaeological discovery. The vast *terra incognita* represented by the Strachey papers seemed like a miniature Pompeii, a whole way of life, that was gradually emerging into the light.
>
> (Penguin edn., p. 17)

Clearly, however questionable its propriety and however scurrilous in some instances, its effects, elementary curiosity has always acted as a primary motivation for the practitioner of biography and a primary source of interest for its readers.

Curiosity, however, has rarely been felt to be justification enough. Biographers, like other literary practitioners, have always felt the need for a moral justification for their activities, and like them they have invariably fallen back on the Horatian formula of pleasure and instruction. 'No part of history is more instructive and delighting than the lives of great and worthy men' wrote Bishop Burnet in 1682 (cit. J. L. Clifford, *Biography as an Art*, London, 1962, p. 13), a sentiment echoed by Dryden, in the passage already referred to, where he assures us that, by comparison with 'history and annals', in pleasure and instruction 'it (i.e. biography) equals, or even excels both of them'. The simplest form of instruction comes, of course, when the subjects of the biographies are themselves figures of blameless credentials: hence Izaak Walton's choice in his *Lives* (1670) of Donne, Wotton, Hooker and Herbert as examples for 'the next age'. The use of biography as a source of moral instruction persisted from the earliest medieval lives of the saints to those tomes of filial piety which Strachey with his famous, if scarcely original analogy, abuses so roundly in his *Eminent Victorians* preface:

> They are as familiar as the cortege of the undertaker and wear the same air of slow funereal barbarism. One is tempted to suppose, of some of them, that they were composed by that functionary, as the final item of his job.
>
> (Penguin edn., p. 10)

Hagiography is an issue to which we shall return: suffice it to say at this point that, in spite of Strachey's strictures, it remains, if hidden under the cloak of scholarly research, as an element to be contended with in the biography of the current century. What are more likely to have changed are the qualifications for canonization.

Independently of the hagiographic instinct, however, the biographer has always felt able to claim that he is concerned with the 'truth': not truth as a philosophical aesthetic concept, as James and Lawrence would have it, but truth in terms of demonstrable fact.

I have already referred to the fact that the earliest novelists were prone to by-pass the charge that their efforts consisted of the creation of falsehood by presenting the careers of their heroes and heroines as if they had actually existed. Defoe may have had his tongue firmly in his cheek when he opened his preface to *Moll Flanders* with a dismissal of the form in which it was written:

> The world is so taken up of late with novels and romances that it will be hard for a private history to be taken for genuine, where the names and other circumstances of the person are concealed,

but the persistence of such devices in less audacious hands, and of the epistolatory form in fiction, shows that that the tradition died hard. A little over a hundred years later, in his review of Croker's edition of Boswell's *Life of Johnson* Carlyle took up the distinction between the novel and biography with a vengeance. Fiction, *sui generis*, he argued, 'partakes, more than we suspect of the nature of *lying*' but, by contrast,

> How inexpressibly comfortable to know our fellow-creature, to see into him, understand his goings-forth, decipher the whole heart of his mystery ... Biography is almost the one thing needful.

What was history, for Carlyle, but 'the essence of innumerable biographies'? Carlyle, of course, was acting under the influence of his own self-immersion in Germanic transcendentalism, with its emphasis on the significance of the self: the kind of truth that he was to obtain from studying the lives of real men was scarcely that arrived at by most modern biographers. It is interesting that when Carlyle came to write his own spiritual autobiography in *Sartor Resartus*, he presented it in the form of a fictional manuscript which a mysterious editor claimed to have discovered. The great rhetorician of truth found himself on this occasion using, if in parodic form, a traditional device of the novel genre which he abominated. But whatever metaphysical ramifications may surround Carlyle's emphasis, the appeal to 'truth' rather than 'fiction' as the basis of a narrative structure has always been one of the heaviest shots in the biographer's locker. Leon Edel, one of the most distinguished of modern biographers, discussing the relationship between biography and psycho-analysis, refers to 'that fine sense of objective inquiry, which both the biographer and the psycho-analyst should – but do not always – cultivate' (cit. Clifford, op. cit., p. 239).

Johnson's 'display' of 'the minutest details of daily life', combined with Edel's 'fine sense of objective inquiry', might seem to provide an ideal formula for the biographer, and certainly, on the face of it, it is a formula that the biographic masterpieces of our own day would seem to have followed. Edel's own five-volume biography of Henry James, Richard Ellman's *James Joyce*, Robert Blake's *Disraeli*, George Painter's *Proust*, Holroyd's *Lytton Strachey* for example, all seem to stand as testimony to such an ideal, in their monumental organisation of the details of their subject's life into a vast total pattern achieved by the detached narrative standpoint. But even here, one is forced to wonder at the degree of detachment. Each of the works cited involved years of patient research bringing author and subject into a relationship of unparalleled intimacy: is it possible, under such circumstances, that the author can stand back as he assembles his material and look at what amounts to a marriage with his subject unaffected by the closeness of the relationship? Edel's phrase a 'fine sense of objective inquiry' has, of itself, a strongly Jamesian ring: in that his work was published over a period of some twenty years it would be surprising indeed if this were not so, but again one is forced to wonder whether, under such circumstances, the scientific method can be sustained unimpaired by the counter-claims of a more complicated attachment to the object of enquiry. And even if we allow the formula as an ideal we should remember that comprehensiveness and objectivity were not always regarded as the touchstones of the biographer's art, and that even when they are, they are not readily attainable. The question that biographers have had to ask themselves in the past has as often been 'how much can the biographer tell?' as 'how much can the biographer know?' The hagiographic as well as the scientific spirit has its problems and it also has produced its masterpieces.

Set against a historical perspective the hagiographic method can be seen at work predominantly in the Renaissance and in Victorian England, and hagiography is an art which creates as many, if not more, problems for its practitioner than scientific investigation. It was North himself who inserted the words 'the Noble' in the title of his translation of Plutarch – *The Lives of The Noble Greeks and Romans*: the *Lives* are in fact moral examples rather than hagiography. If we are given Alexander and Julius Caesar as examples of a particular virtue we also have Alcibiades and Coriolanus to warn us against inherent flaws of personality. Dealing with classical figures, North was on safe ground, but for the Elizabethans biography was often identifiably interwoven with history and the propagandist biographer would have to move cautiously when approaching more contemporary figures. For his Victorian equivalent the problem was rather different: here the danger was not so much political as domestic. 'Truth' was a Victorian ideal, but so too was discretion and the prolific output of Victorian biography reveals all too readily the strain between these conflicting virtues. In this respect certain aspects of human personality, most notably those relating to sexual behaviour, were obviously forbidden ground. The problem was intensified by the fact that the biographer was often commissioned by the family, if he was not indeed a member of it, and it was not unusual for him to act as literary executor as well. The roles could often conflict: we know for example that Ruskin's literary executors destroyed much of his more interesting correspondence in order to avert the danger of biographical exposure. How could a man like Arthur Penrhyn Stanley, Thomas Arnold's own prize pupil, detach himself in any way from his subject when he had been commissioned to write the official life by the Doctor's widow while in attendance on the family mourning, or Mrs Kingsley compile a life of her husband, the novelist and reformer, without performing extensive acts of editorial surgery? But the partiality imposed by such circumstances did not necessarily lead to disaster. Stanley's *Arnold*, despite dismissals by unsympathetic critics, is by no means an unreadable account of a great man's life, while Mrs Gaskell's *Life of Charlotte Brontë*, commissioned under more testing circumstances, but still on the grounds of the author's closeness to its subject, has always been acknowledged as a masterpiece of the genre. No one can have felt more intensely the predicament of the commemorative biographer than Mrs Gaskell but she was guided throughout by her determination to make her appeal 'to that larger and more solemn public, who know how to admire generously extraordinary genius, and how to reverence with warm, full hearts all noble virtue' (*The Life of Charlotte Brontë*, Penguin edn., ed. Alan Shelston, p. 526). The statement of priorities is unashamedly that of the advocate rather than the judge, and it is not difficult for the modern scholar to demonstrate the selectivity of Mrs Gaskell's method and the partiality of her commentary, but the greatness of the work itself remains to remind us that objectivity is not the only standard by which the success of a biographer may be measured, and that closeness between author and subject – 'my dear friend Charlotte Brontë' – as Mrs Gaskell called her at the outset – can have its positive advantages, not the least of which is a familiarity of personal knowledge and understanding which no amount of academic research can replace.

The modern biographer may feel free of the question of how much he should tell (although Holroyd himself is obliged to quote Strachey's 'Discretion is not the better part of biography' in his own preface as justification for his own activities). How much the biographer can know is more likely to be his major concern. The sources on which he must call need to be searched for: always there will be the hope, possibly the fear, that further material will be unearthed to extend the comprehensiveness of his account or to disturb his developing pattern. Furthermore the biographer cannot always expect the complicity of his chosen subject. Ernest Jones, in his *Life and Work of Sigmund Freud*, quotes a letter which reveals

how his own task was complicated by the action of Freud himself
(then aged twenty-eight):

> I have just carried out one resolution (writes Freud) which one
> group of people as yet unborn and fated to misfortune, will feel
> acutely. Since you can't guess who I mean I will tell you: they
> are my biographers. I have destroyed all my diaries of the past
> fourteen years, with letters, scientific notes and the manuscripts
> of any publications ... Let the biographers chafe; we won't make
> it too easy for them. Let each one of them believe he is right
> in his 'Conception of the Development of the Hero': even now
> I enjoy the thought of how they will all go astray.
>
> (Penguin edn., abridged and edited by Lionel Trilling
> and Steven Marcus, pp. 26–7)

Freud, in fact, was only following the tradition of many of his
English predecessors in the nineteenth century whose gardens
would seem at times to have been ablaze with the correspondence
that they wished to preserve from the investigations of posterity.
The thinness of our knowledge of Shakespeare's life is notorious,
and the time factor must inevitably be a strong one in the search
for evidence. But if Shakespeare has his dark lady, Matthew Arnold
has his Marguerite, while modern biographers, provoked by their
predecessors, still debate the nature of the relationship between
Carlyle and his wife.

But even if we grant our ideal biographer complete freedom of
access to his sources, intimacy with his subject coupled with
detachment in his account, independence of taboos, and moral and
political objectivity, it remains impossible to evade the ultimate
question about the nature of the truth that he tells. When Aubrey
writes of the supernatural torments of one Francis Fry that,

> returning from work (that little he can do) he was caught by
> the Woman Spectre by the Skirts of his Doublet and carried
> into the Air

and goes on to record

> That the Daemon carried him so high that he saw his Master's
> House underneath him no bigger than a Hay-cock
>
> (*Brief Lives*, Penguin edn., pp. 270–1)

we are inclined to dismiss him as either credulous, or deliberately
sensationalist. In fact, of course, Aubrey was recounting what to
him may well have seemed to be the truth: in a century when
a king had published a volume on demonology it was not unreasonable for a biographer to accept the existence of spirits. And
if we feel ourselves to be superior to this kind of 'truth' we have
only to refer to Ernest Jones's account of the efficacy of Freud's
treatment of Gustav Mahler, with whom he spent just one four-
hour session walking the streets of Leyden:

> Although Mahler had had no previous contact with psycho-
> analysis, Freud said he had never met anyone who seemed to
> understand it so swiftly. Mahler was greatly impressed by a
> remark of Freud's: 'I take it that your mother was called Marie.
> I should surmise it from various hints in your conversation. How
> came it that you married someone with another name, Alma,
> since your mother evidently played a dominating part in your
> life? Mahler then told him that his wife's name was Alma Maria
> but that he called her Marie! She was the daughter of the famous
> painter (in German 'Mahler') Schindler, whose statue stands in
> the Stadtpark in Vienna; so presumably a name played a part
> in her life also. This analytic talk evidently produced an effect,
> since Mahler recovered his potency and the marriage was a happy
> one until his death, which unfortunately took place only a year
> later.
>
> (op. cit., pp. 358–9)

Perhaps only a totally committed Freudian like Jones could have
produced that final sentence without a glimmer of humour, but
the example serves to show just how strongly the truth of the
biographer, like that of the historian, must depend upon the intellectual climate of his age. Not all twentieth-century biography is
explicitly Freudian, of course, but it lives in Freud's shadow.

Acceptance of the formative influence of childhood experience is inherent in most post-Romantic biographical writing: re-inforced by Freud's authority the tendency to deploy, if only implicitly, the methods of psychological analysis is evident throughout the present age. By analogy the Marxist will seek to explain human behaviour in terms of the irresistible processes of history, for biography of its nature cannot stop at factual record: instinctively it must move on to explanation and interpretation.

The biographer who aims at completeness will seek to find, in his mass of facts, actions and patterns of behaviour which will contribute to a consistent explanation of the overall life of his subject. Thus, in the earliest chapters of his monumental study, *Hitler, a Study in Tyranny* (1952), Alan Bullock has already identified the sources of Hitler's anti-Semitism, his detestation of socialism, and his Germanic nationalism, while refuting Hitler's self-created mythology of his early life in *Mein Kampf*. The method is more deliberately organised, but no different in kind from that of Boswell who writes in his introductory chapter to *The Life of Johnson* that 'there is here an illustration of intelligence from various points, by which his character is more fully understood and illustrated'. 'Understood', implicitly by the reader, but the process of illustration is conducted by Boswell himself, and the proliferation of lives of Johnson that followed Boswell's own work would at least seem to suggest that his contemporaries had differing views about Johnson's character and career. One of the more remarkable aspects of *The Life of Johnson* is its anticipation of modern biography, particularly in its combination of comprehensiveness and an interpretative impulse that never imposes itself on the reader.

I have concentrated in this introductory survey on biography which, whatever the limitations imposed upon it by the conventions of its age, or by the accessibility of source-materials, has operated in terms of identifiable and assessable detail and in which the methodology has been generally cumulative and the objective a certain comprehensiveness. The biographer, as I have suggested however, does not simply narrate, he interprets as well, and there has always been a tendency in biography to select in order to interpret – to select and perhaps even to invent. How many of those famous last words, for example, really passed the lips of the biographical subject *in extremis*? According to Hesketh Pearson, in his biography of Oscar Wilde, the dying Wilde was heard to complain of the wallpaper in his dingy Parisian hotel. 'It is killing me,' Wilde is reported as having said, 'One of us *had* to go'. Philippe Jullian, another of Wilde's biographers, gives us the same story, with a slight verbal variation, and yet there is something about its very appropriateness that makes us wonder whether it is not part of an inherited mythology rather than a provable fact. Whatever reliability we may feel able to place in it, however, we would not want to give it up, for it seems such an ideal story with which to conclude the life of such a man.

The most objective of biographers have always used the technique of stressing the particular significance of individual instances of human behaviour, but it has been left to a minority to represent the whole by so deliberate a selection of the parts as to produce a biographical mood that is impressionistic rather than historical. The result is often closer to fiction than to biography as conventionally considered. Lytton Strachey is the most obvious example of a biographer who works in this way, but he has contemporary support from the unlikely figure of Norman Mailer. Contemplating the problems of writing a life of Marilyn Monroe he writes:

> It is possible there is no instrument more ready to capture the elusive quality of her nature than a novel. Set a thief to catch a thief, and put an artist on an artist. Could the solution be nothing less vainglorious than a novel of Marilyn Monroe? Written in the form of biography?
>
> (Norman Mailer, *Marilyn*, London, 1973)

This chapter started with the novelist's claim that fiction, by its freedom to select, could offer the highest form of truth. The impressionistic biographer might similarly claim that his impressions, however doubtful their authenticity, are capable of achieving a truth more instinctive, and thus more intrinsic, than the facts of the compiler and chronicler, however skilfully deployed. W. H. Auden has a poem, 'Who's Who', which begins, 'A shilling life will give you all the facts', and it is impossible to miss the element of contempt in that opening line. Once again the artist and the biographer find themselves in conflict.

When jesting Pilate speculated on the nature of truth he took the practical course of dismissing the question, and it is very doubtful whether the biographer could have resolved it for him:

> There's always something one's ignorant of
> About anyone, however well one knows them;
> And that may be something of the greatest importance.
> It's when you're sure you understand a person
> That you're liable to make the worst mistake about him.

What Sir Claude Mulholland offers in *The Confidential Clerk* as a fact about the limitations of our understanding of human character might well be taken as a motto for the aspiring biographer. In the chapters which follow I aim to explore some of the ways in which biographers have set about their impossible task, and I have done so by examining particular examples within a chronological context. I have done this not to offer a history of the form – in the space available such an objective would obviously be unattainable – but because I believe that any biography is inextricably linked with the priorities and assumptions of the age which produced it. My examples, like the facts of the biographer, will necessarily be selective, for with biography, as with any other literary form, it is only by close investigation of the individual work that one can begin to understand the processes that go into its creation.

2

Exemplum and anecdote

In *The Advancement of Learning*, published in 1605, Francis Bacon
reflected on the paucity of biographical writing in his own day:

> For lives, I do find strange that these times have so little esteemed
> the virtues of the times, as that the writings of the lives should
> be no more frequent. For although there be not many sovereign
> princes or absolute commanders, and that States are most col-
> lected into monarchies, yet are there many worthy personages
> that deserve better than disperst report or barren elogies.
>
> (Everyman edn., p. 95)

'Disperst report' and 'barren elogies' are phrases which aptly describe a great deal of such biography as had found its way into print
during the Elizabethan period, but Bacon's complaint is based, in
fact, on an attempt to categorise 'history' which, he tells us, 'either
representeth a time, or a person, or an action'. It was the second
category which Bacon found deficient, but if we adopt a less rigid
approach to the inter-relationship of biography and history it would
seem that Bacon – who himself was to write a *Life of Henry VII*
(history or biography?) – was perhaps over-severe on the biographical efforts of his contemporaries.

The paths of history and biography obviously have a tendency
to converge but they are particularly difficult to distinguish in the
sixteenth and seventeenth centuries. As a coherent historiography
develops during this period so do techniques of biography, and
if any one element can be said to account for the closeness of the
relationship it must have been the developing awareness that human

history was as much a consequence of human actions as of divine disposition. Carlyle's assertion that history is a compound of individual biographies would have seemed so obvious to the historians of the Renaissance as not to need saying. The inheritance of the Renaissance historian was moralistic: the great events of the past were cited as warnings and guidance for the conduct of the present. The conduct, however, was that of individual men. *The Mirrour for Magistrates* (1559), a long collection of exemplary political careers in verse was essentially moralistic in its emphasis but it makes a crucial point about the responsibility of the historian:

> But seeing causes are the chiefest things
> That should be noted of the story writers
> That men may learn what ends all causes brings
> They be unworthy of the name of Chroniclers
> That leave these clean out of their registers.

The emphasis on 'causes' is something new: the anonymous author is as much interested in *why* people had behaved as they did as in *what* they had actually done.

In North's translation of Plutarch's *Lives* (1579), itself taken from the French version of Jacques Amyot published some twenty years earlier, the pattern is projected into the future. Translating Amyot's preface, the substance of which he endorses, North tells us that

> an historie is an orderly register of notable things sayd, done, or happened in tyme past, to mainteyne the continuall remembrance of them, and to serve for the instruction of them to come.

For North, as for the anonymous author of *The Mirrour for Magistrates*, the most telling form of history was the biographical, hence the admiration for Plutarch which he records in his own prefatory note 'To the Reader':

> For all others were fayne to take their matter, as the fortune of the contries whereof they wrote fell out: But this man being excellent in wit, learning and experience, hath chosen the speciall

actes of the best persons, of the famosest nations of the world.

Here, indeed, North follows the priorities of his hero, who in the *Life of Alexander* declared that 'my intent is not to write histories but only lives', but for the Elizabethan writer the distinction is not so clear-cut.

The modern historian, of course, would look for causation in other areas besides the behaviour of individuals, but for his Elizabethan counterpart the search tended to stop there. The methodology of history may, as J. R. Hale has pointed out, have made a dramatic advance when 'the work of the generation of writers from Stow to Selden established once and for all that documents and not secondary authorities are the essential foundations of reliable history' (*The Evolution of British Historiography*, London, 1967, p. 11) but the new humanism ensured that history remained a matter of the examination of the past in terms of the conduct of individuals rather than, for example, economic, demographic or even, despite the development of antiquarianism, topographical forces. Thus it is that any attempt in the Renaissance to distinguish, as Bacon does, between biography and history is foredoomed since they are inter-related aspects of the same area and spirit of enquiry. The chroniclers, the annalists, the antiquarians may not have been biographers in the modern sense, but one might query to what extent, in the modern sense, they were historians.

This is, of course, even more true of the examples of such history and biography as may be drawn from the medieval past. Biography has its lives of the saints: history its chroniclers, and both organised their largely legendary material in the service of a providential rather than a humanistically orientated concept of human events. Similarly, just as the Tudor historian, initially at least, put propaganda before probity, so did, for example, the author (usually considered to be Sir Thomas More) of the anonymous *History of Richard III* (1517), whatever the merits of its dramatic presentation of its subject-matter. Here it is interesting to note that the only two native works written in the Tudor period which have been generally accepted as precursors of modern biography, George Cavendish's *Life of Cardinal Wolsey* and William Roper's *Life of Sir Thomas More*, were not published until well into the seventeenth century. The subjects of both works were figures of contention: again there would seem to be a link between the Elizabethans, and their Victorian successors, for whom discretion, if for rather different reasons, had a tendency to inhibit publication. As Raleigh remarked in the introduction to his *History of the World*, 'Whosoever, in writing a moderne Historie shall follow truth too neare the heeles, it may haply strike out his teeth.'

Contemporary lives, like contemporary events, might prove dangerous to the Elizabethan commentator. The events of the distant past however, provided safer ground, hence the success of the various translations not only of Plutarch, but of other classical authorities. Analogy with Shakespearian drama helps to make the point. In those plays which deal with English history Shakespeare provides – although I would argue that the strain often shows – a predominantly traditionalist view of history, organised towards a coherent conclusion. In Shakespeare's Roman plays however, one finds not conclusive statements of political theory but far more open-ended forms of debate: the difference is indicated as clearly in their structure as it is in the stories of the drama. It may indeed be coincidental, but the organisation of Plutarch's *Lives*, with its deliberate pairing of Greek and Roman examples, its comparative essays on the examples chosen and its careful choice of those examples to reveal a range of human behaviour, leaves us with the sense that I think we get from those plays in which Shakespeare drew so heavily on Plutarch – a sense of the openness of the possibilities of human behaviour as much as a deliberate organisation of that behaviour to provide an acceptable political morality. The remarkable thing about Plutarch's *Lives* is that whatever moralistic purpose their original author may have intended – or his translators may have emphasised – one is aware all the time of a fascination about the details of human behaviour that cannot be constrained within the limits of a purely exemplary

scheme. Plutarch's Marcus Antonius may be a less attractive character than Shakespeare's Antony, and the fact that he is paired with
Demetrius, whose career followed a similar pattern of achievement
and self-destruction, is an indication of how we are meant to think
of him. But Plutarch, just as much as Shakespeare, stresses
Antony's largesse, his nobility of appearance, his capacities of
endurance and, in the best sense, his personal carelessness in a
way that shows, as does Shakespeare's play, how Antony's decline
was a consequence as much of the dualistic nature of his personal
characteristics – 'those very things that procured him ill-repute
bear witness to his greatness', Plutarch concludes in his essay comparing Antony with Demetrius – as of any inherent evil in him.

> And in the end, 'the horse of the mind', as Plato termeth it,
> that is so hard of rein (I mean the unreined lust of concupiscence),
> did put out Antonius' head all honest and commendable
> thoughts,

is Plutarch's ultimate judgement on Antony, but the 'in the end'
is the crucial phrase. Mark Antony's life is certainly a cautionary
tale, but it is by no means an uncomplicated one, and what one
finds in Plutarch's *Lives*, and indeed what distinguishes them from
so much exemplary biography, is exactly that sense of the complexity of human character which it is the responsibility of the
biographer to unravel.

For all the careful organisation of his work, Plutarch would seem
to be as much interested in incident and, in particular in those
incidents which reveal aspects of character, as in providing moral
example. Dealing in *The Life of Julius Caesar* with Caesar's rejection of his wife Pompeia for suspicion of adultery with her lover
Clodius he writes:

> Thus notwithstanding, Caesar presently put his wife away; and
> thereupon, being brought by Clodius' accuser to be a witness
> against him, he answered he knew nothing of that they objected
> against Clodius. This answer being clean contrary to their expec-

tation that heard it, the accuser asked Caesar why, then, he had put away his wife.

'Because I will not,' said he 'that my wife be as much as suspected.' And some say that Caesar spake truly as he thought. But others think that he did it to please the common people, who were very desirous to save Clodius.

Two points are of interest here. Plutarch has taken a famous incident in Caesar's history and seized on it as fascinating evidence of a distinctive aspect of his character. Having done so, however, he offers two interpretations of Caesar's action (neither of them to our eyes particularly creditable perhaps) but then leaves the issue at that. As with the case of Mark Antony, the parallel life (that of Alexander) is an indication of the general purpose that the life of Caesar is meant to serve, although in this case there is no comparative essay. The example again shows however that Plutarch's biographical technique is by no means as simplistic as the overtly expository stance implicit in the structure of the work as a whole would suggest, and which the Renaissance translators, acting under the influence of the priorities of their own age, assumed so readily.

In discussing Plutarch's *Lives* I have referred throughout to North's translation and the pitfalls involved in such a practice are obvious enough. North's *Plutarch*, like Chapman's *Homer* was so much a work of its period, distanced not only in time but in stance, from its original that we sometimes tend to forget its proper ancestry. Just how much the language and attitudes of the age affect the translation can be seen if we compare North's version, published in 1579, with that supervised by Dryden which appeared just over a hundred years later in 1683. The problem is compounded by the fact that, as I have indicated, the work is a translation of a translation. We should not, however, allow ourselves to be too strongly deterred by this problem. As an incidental compensation we have the vigour of North's own vernacular which adds force to his narrative, as when he tells us, for example, that Brutus 'was

yet but a stripling or springal of twenty years old', or that
Antony's house 'within was full of tumblers, antic dancers, jugglers,
players, jesters and drunkards, quaffing and guzzling'. More im-
portantly North's translation made Plutarch available to his contemporaries, and indeed to us, as a classical precedent for biography
as a form in its own right, by-passing the whole corpus of medieval
hagiography. Furthermore its contemporary popularity, arising in
the first place from the generally revived interest in the classics,
but more specifically from a developing awareness of the significance of individual lives seen within a political, as distinct from
a religious, framework, serves to remind us that biography can
come in many forms. Bacon was able to argue that biography had
not developed as might have been expected, because his innate
tendency to categorise had produced a category with few examples.
Plutarch's *Lives* make it clear that if we are less rigid about the
division between biography and history the argument fails to stand,
and to history we might well add the drama, and indeed the
narrative poetry of the period as legitimate sources for the study
of biography. It may be true that the actual term 'biography' was
not in current usage until the middle of the seventeenth century
but we should remember that it was Polonius who specified the
categories of the drama and the players who performed the play.
The Elizabethans may not have produced biography in a form
which would satisfy formulaic requirements, but the emphasis
placed by so much of their literature on the stories of individual
lives bears ample testimony to the existence of the biographical
temper in the period.

The connection between history and biography did not cease
with the emergence of a more scholarly historical methodology.
As I have indicated, the priorities of the historian at this time
tended to move from the moralistic emphasis of the exemplum to
the more agnostic approach of the antiquarian survey. Camden's
Brittania (1586) was one of the earliest of such works and it set
the pattern for later developments like Thomas Fuller's *The
Worthies of England* (1662) and the researches of the Oxford anti-

...iom we owe the existence of Aubrey's
...utline obviously cannot do justice to
...istoriography – it completely ignores
...eigh's unfinished *History of the World*,
...kind – but it does serve to show the
...in biography to those in the related
...work was in fact an account primarily
of the ... ...man and Anglo-Saxon Britain, but to
achieve his object he ...s us that,

> I have travelled almost all over England and have consulted in
> each county the persons of best skill and knowledge in these
> matters. . . . I have examined the public records of the kingdom,
> ecclesiastical registers and libraries, and the acts, monuments
> and memorials of churches and cities.

Fuller, in the opening paragraph of his 'Design of the Ensuing
Work' refers back to 'learned Master Camden and painful Master
Speed', and in his survey of the England of his own day he
included the biographical element:

> I confess, the subject is but dull in itself, to tell the time and
> places of men's birth, and deaths, their names, with the names
> and number of their books: and therefore this bare skeleton of
> time, place and person must be fleshed with some pleasant pass-
> ages. To this intent I have purposely interlaced (not as meat,
> but as condiment) many delightful stories.

Fuller's title, *The Worthies of England*, bears witness to the continuing influence of the exemplary tradition – whatever interpretation might be placed on the term 'worthy' it could scarcely have
been applied to some of Aubrey's subjects. But this is now combined
with the antiquarian tradition in which Aubrey, working in the
final decades of the seventeenth century, found himself, and while
he was never able to co-ordinate his multifarious talents so far as
to achieve publication in his own day it is clear from his own
records, compiled for us by Oliver Lawson Dick, that his exuberant

curiosity is in fact that of the born antiquarian, harvesting and harbouring whatever came to hand in his researches into the topography and family history of the England of the seventeenth century.

If Aubrey's work can be traced directly to his antiquarian activities its mode of expression reminds us of another influence, that of the glut of autobiographical writing that appeared in the seventeenth century. Like the rise of biography, the similar developments in autobiography are a consequence of the new humanism, and as does biography, the autobiography of the period appears in a variety of scarcely definable forms. That of the diary is the form of which we are reminded by Aubrey, and one of the more remarkable aspects of Aubrey's *Brief Lives* is the way in which we are constantly made aware of the range of the author's acquaintance. Repeatedly he is able to state that he knew his subject personally or at one remove: he has that degree of intimacy with his subject-matter which reminds us of Pepys and which we are later to associate with Boswell. Aubrey has a totally different objective from Boswell, and nothing of his single-mindedness of purpose but, like Boswell, he reminds us very clearly of the advantages accruing to the biographer who has been personally acquainted with his subject, and which in his case at least allows us to accept the most astonishing inprobabilities in the spirit of truth.

The motivation and the methodology of the antiquarian and the diarist are both very similar: they are inspired by an active interest in human experience and they work in terms of accumulation rather than organisation. Aubrey's *Brief Lives* are entirely anecdotal: he records his discoveries with a delightful freshness that has lost nothing for the modern reader. However he rarely goes behind the anecdote to investigate the deeper aspects of human character, and neither does he organise his recollections into a consistent framework which would enable us to see his characters whole. Consider, for example, his story of Mr Caisho Burroughs:

Mr Caisho Burroughs was one of the most beautiful men in

England, and very valiant, but very proud and blood-thirsty: There was then in London a very beautiful Italian Lady, who fell so extremely in Love with him, that she did let him enjoy her, which she had never let any Man do before: Wherefore, said she, I shall request this favour of you, never to tell anyone of it. The Gentlewoman died: and afterwards in a Tavern in London he spake of it: and there going to make water, the Ghost of the Gentlewoman did appear to him. He was afterwards troubled with the apparition of her, even sometimes in company when he was drinking; but he only perceived it: Before she did appear he did find a kind of Chiliness upon his spirits.

(*Brief Lives*, Penguin edn., p. 191)

This is a splendid story, and it loses nothing from the fact that we are bound to see it as a very tall one, whereas there is no reason why Aubrey should have done so. But the story in itself tells us very little about Mr Caisho Burroughs: his pride is recorded, as is a very appropriate nemesis, but one could scarcely talk in more than the most elementary terms of anything approaching a comprehensive study of character. And if it be objected that Burroughs is only worthy of record because of his one very singular experience it has to be said that even where Aubrey deals with figures who have rather more to recommend them, and is himself aware of it, he always deploys an anecdotal method which offers an impressionistic rather than an analytic approach to character. When he tells us, for example of Sir Francis Bacon that:

His Lordship would often drinke a good draught of strong Beer (March-beer) to-bedwards, to lay his worthy Fancy asleep which otherwise would keep him from sleeping great part of the night,

(Penguin edn., p. 175)

we are made graphically aware of the kind of intellectual restlessness that lay behind Bacon's philosophical achievements, but from there we move to an account of the splendours of Verulam, before the appropriate anecdote of the manner of Bacon's death as a result of an experiment in refrigeration. Aubrey is obviously fascinated by Bacon, and he respects him, but his fall from office, which one might think would be a crucial matter for investigation, is simply recorded as having occurred. The same might be said of his account of Sir Walter Raleigh, although in this case there is a greater awareness of the fact that he is dealing with a career whose meteoric course is worthy of investigation for reasons beyond that of narrative attractiveness. Even here though we tend to remember the Raleigh who 'loved a wench well ... getting one of the Mayds of Honour against a tree in a Wood' or the Raleigh who 'did not care to goe on the Thames in a Wherry-boat (but) would rather goe round about over London bridg' as much as the courtier and statesman whose fall was an object of wonder to his contemporaries.

> He took a pipe of Tobacco a little before he went to the
> scaffold, which some formall persons were scandalised at, but
> I think 'twas well and properly done, to settle his spirits
>
> (Penguin edn., p. 422)

Aubrey tells us, and indeed only Aubrey would have introduced the account of Raleigh's execution in quite such a way; if the life ends on a properly reflective note it is the observed detail, rather than the philosophical observation that stands in our mind.

To insist that Aubrey's virtues are those of the impressionist rather than the analyst is not necessarily to make a value-judgement. We might feel that an analytic mind might have offered us a more categoric insight into human character but it could scarcely have provided so consistently the sense of lives in the actual process of being lived that we get from the *Brief Lives*. The differences between Plutarch and Aubrey are too obvious to need exposition, but they both have the biographer's capacity for total immersion in the day-to-day experience of the people whose lives they recall. And here again the relationship between the biographer and the historian becomes interwoven. North translated Plutarch's *Lives* for his contemporaries in the spirit of exemplification which suited both Plutarch's purposes and his own. From Aubrey we get a different kind of record: for all his apparent credulity, he offers us the spirit of the modern, and he offers it with a confidence coming from his absolute faith that he is living in an age of infinite possibilities. We sense a particularly good example of this in his record of the career of Sir William Petty. The opening sentence tells us that 'His father was by profession a clothier, and also did dye his owne cloathes: he left little or no estate to Sir William.' Petty becomes a linguist, a mathematician, an anatomist who 'reads Vesalius with Mr. Thomas Hobbes, who loved his company', and ultimately a surveyor and inventor. At Oxford:

> he taught Anatomy to the young Scholars. Anatomy was then but little understood by the university, and I remember he kept a body that he brought by water from Reding a good while to read upon some way soused or pickled. About these times Experimentall Philosophy first budded here and was first cultivated by these Vertuosi in the darke time.

> (Penguin edn., p. 399)

In a passage such as this biography becomes history in a particularly distinctive way: we are able to experience the pride which Aubrey, one of the first Fellows of the Royal Society in 1663, felt in his age. It was an age of class mobility and intellectual achievement, and this is made abundantly clear by the way in which Aubrey is able to record the humble origins of so many of his characters who rose to social and intellectual stature, and by the particular admiration which he feels for figures like Robert Boyle, 'that profound Philosopher, accomplished Humanist and Excellent Divine', William Harvey 'Inventor of the Circulation of the Blood' – 'Ah! My old friend Dr. Harvey – I knew him right well' – and Thomas Hobbes, another personal friend. The most immediate attractions of Aubrey are his love of anecdote and the uncritical freshness of his prose. His lasting qualities however are those not of a biographer of individuals but of a recorder of the social and intellectual movements of an age. If, by Aubrey's time, biography can be said to be in the debt of history, he can be said to have done much to repay that debt.

This chapter has been primarily concerned to examine the relationship between biography and history, and in doing so it has by-passed a considerable amount of biographical writing produced in the seventeenth century. At this time, for example, the literary 'character', an adjunct of that enthusiasm for reporting which gave rise to so much recorded reminiscence, became almost a literary form in its own right. Distinguishable from this rather amorphous collection of biographical material, both in terms of quality and kind, is Izaak Walton's *Lives*, i.e. of Donne, Wotton, Hooker and Herbert, initially published separately, but later collected in a single volume in 1670. (Walton was later to publish a fifth life, that of Robert Sanderson, Bishop of Lincoln, in 1678.)

Walton's *Lives* are often referred to as the first examples of English biography which possess genuinely literary merit in their own right. Be that as it may, they are of particular interest in terms of the polarities suggested by North's *Plutarch* and Aubrey's *Brief Lives* for they represent a continuation of the exemplary mode and the anecdotal method, substantiated in this instance by the discursive deployment of documentary evidence. The subjects of Walton's *Lives* were very different from those of both North and Aubrey, although Aubrey himself does give a respectful account of George Herbert. Walton inscribed his title-page with a text from Ecclesiastes: 'These were honourable men in their Generations' and of Herbert's life he writes 'if it were related by a pen like his there would be no need for this Age to look back into times past for examples of primitive piety'. While the lives were written separately it can scarcely have been a coincidence that Walton chose as his subjects four distinguished clerics, three of whom, Donne, Wotton and Herbert provided added exemplary weight by the fact that they had each rejected in their various ways 'ambitious desires and the outward Glory of this World' for lives of contemplation. Of Donne's initial resistance to holy orders Walton writes:

This was his present resolution; but, the heart of one man is not in his own keeping; and he was destined to this sacred service by a higher hand, a hand so powerful, as at last forced him to a compliance: of which I shall give the Reader an account before I shall give a rest to my Pen.

(Walton's *Lives*, World's Classics edn., p. 35)

The more equitable Wotton, after an energetic life of travel and public service, becomes a devout Provost of Eton whose orthodoxy made him 'a great enemy to wrangling Disputes of religion', while the account of Herbert's transition from courtier to saintly parish priest has initiated a legend. Walton's later *Life of Sanderson* repeats the tendencies of the first four lives: Sanderson, another contemporary of Walton, preserved his integrity of conscience throughout the religious ferment of the Civil War and achieved his bishopric at the age of seventy-three, but he too is presented as a lover of 'obscure and quiet privacy' who 'either found or made his Parishioners peaceable and complying with him in the decent and regular service of God'. Of Walton's subjects only Hooker was marked out for the highest ecclesiastical distinction from his earliest days, and it is clear that in this instance, in which Walton deals with a prestigious theologian of the past, he was motivated by rather different considerations from those which applied in the other cases, and indeed produced a rather different kind of biography.

The recurrent pattern of Walton's biographical priorities is not such as to impose a rigidly moralistic structure on his work. Indeed such structure as we find is, one suspects, accidental rather than imposed. Throughout the *Lives* we are reminded of the power of the 'higher hand' of Providence: thus, introducing the description of Herbert's conflict with himself about his ultimate calling, Walton refers instinctively to 'God, in whom there is an unseen Chain of Causes', but the piety is always humanised, firstly by the use of anecdote to reveal the nature of the biographical subject, and secondly by the intimacy of tone of Walton's accounts. If the method is demonstrably partial in its emphasis on the spirituality of the lives depicted – all of Walton's figures are writers themselves, three of them poets, but he usually refers to their literary works only in passing – its authenticity springs from the very close affinity between author and subject. We find it perhaps most consistently deployed in the *Life of Herbert*, notably in the account of Herbert's relationship with his mother and in the reverent but never obsequious description of Herbert's conduct of the living of Bemerton, but effective examples are to be found throughout the *Lives*. Here, for example, is Walton's description of Wotton's regimen at Eton:

> And now to speak a little of the imployment of his time in the Colledge. After his customary publick Devotions, his use was to retire into his *Study*, and there to spend some hours in reading the Bible, and Authors in Divinity, closing up his meditations with private prayer; this was for the most part, his imployment in the Forenoon: But when he was once sate to Dinner, then nothing but cheerful thoughts possess'd his mind; and those still increased by constant company at his Table, of such persons as brought thither additions both of Learning and Pleasure; but some part of most days was usually spent in *Philosophical Conclusions*. Nor did he forget his innate pleasure of *Angling*, which he would often call, *his idle time, not idly spent*; saying often, he would rather live *five May* months, than *forty Decembers*.
>
> (World's Classics edn., p. 130)

Here we have example, illustrated by anecdote, and an intimacy of tone springing from the close sympathy of the biographer for his subject. Close relationships, of course, are not always as happy as those revealed by Walton's *Lives*, neither do they always make for effective biography. The nature of the author–subject relationship however is a crucial factor in the study of the form: the choice and treatment of a subject can reveal as much about the biographer as the biography may reveal of the subject itself.

3

Author and subject

Walton's predilection for writing about people with whose virtues he was personally acquainted set a pattern which was to be repeated in many of the great biographies of our literature. In his preface to *The Life of Sanderson* he indicates his use of a technique that Boswell, the greatest of biographers, was to refine to the point where it became the hallmark of his biographic method. Referring to his wish to preserve Sanderson's memory he writes:

> I desire to tell the Reader, that in this Relation I have been so bold, as to paraphrase and say what I think he (whom I had the happiness to know well) would have said upon the same occasions.

> (World's Classics edn., p. 345)

Boswell was to go a stage further, in that he tenaciously recorded Dr Johnson's conversation at the time of utterance, but in Walton's statement we see prefigured a means of achieving biographic authenticity that is a direct consequence of intimacy between author and subject. Such intimacy has wide implications for biography as a form, and in this chapter I propose to examine the nature of the relationship between the biographer and his subject in the two major classics of eighteenth-century biography, Johnson's *Life of Mr Richard Savage* (1744) and Boswell's *Life of Samuel Johnson* (1791).

Johnson himself has a particular centrality for the student of biography. We know him as biographical subject primarily through Boswell's *Life*, and as a practitioner through the *Life of Savage*

and *The Lives of the Poets*. In each aspect, however, these are only
the primary manifestations of Johnson's significance. His attractions as a biographical subject appealed not only to Boswell, but
also to Sir John Hawkins and Mrs Thrale, and the list only begins
with these names. Throughout Boswell's *Life* we sense his awareness that his version of Johnson is not the only one in circulation.
It is with as much glee as sympathy, for example, that he describes
Hawkins, on one instance as 'unlucky on all occasions' and his
sensitivity to the need to adopt a protective stance towards Johnson
springs not simply from a need to account for the more awkward
aspects of his character but from the realisation that his hero is
a common topic of discussion and report. A recent compilation
entitled *The Early Biographies of Samuel Johnson* (ed. O. M. Brock,
Jr. and Robert E. Kelley, Iowa City, 1974) gives us fourteen
biographical sources for Johnson dating from 1762, the year when
Boswell first met Johnson, to 1786, a year after Johnson's death,
and while many of these are only brief notices they testify very
clearly to the interest that Johnson had for his contemporaries.
David Erskine Baker, writing in 1764, describes Johnson as 'no
less the Glory of the present Age and Nation, than he will be the
Admiration of all succeeding ones' (Brock and Kelley, op. cit., p. 5).
Few such contemporary claims have proved to be so accurate. As
for Johnson's own performance as a biographer it has been
estimated by John Butt that 'the grand and almost formidable total'
of Johnson's biographical writings is sixty-three. (*Biography in the
Hands of Walton, Johnson and Boswell*, Los Angeles, 1966, p. 19.)
Again many of these items are occasional pieces, but they testify
to the importance that biography, as a literary form, had not only
for Johnson but for his contemporaries.

Johnson's views on biography are clearly expressed in two essays,
The Rambler, No. 60 and *The Idler*, No. 84. The particular
distinction of the form for Johnson arises from the fact that it
affords an easily assimilable source of moral instruction and com-
fort. It is, 'of the various kinds of narrative writing, that which
is most eagerly read, and most easily applied to the purposes of

life' (*Idler*, 84). The point is put more fully in *The Rambler* essay:

> I have often thought that there has rarely passed a life of which
> a judicious and faithful narrative would not be useful. For, not
> only every man has, in the mighty mass of the world, great
> numbers in the same condition with himself, to whom his
> mistakes and miscarriages, escapes and expedients, would be of
> immediate and apparent use; but there is such a uniformity in
> the state of man, considered apart from adventitious and separ-
> able decorations and disguises, that there is scarce any possibility
> of good or ill but is common to human kind.

Johnson's attitude towards biography is thus essentially moralistic,
but it follows from his argument that moral improvement is to
be gained not necessarily from great events – 'those performances
and incidents, which produce vulgar greatness' – but from
'domestic privacies (and) the minute details of daily life' (*Rambler*,
No. 60). It follows also that biography can only be undertaken
by a close acquaintance of the subject, writing at a point in time
not far removed from the subject's life:

> If a life be delayed till interest and envy are at an end, we may
> hope for impartiality, but must expect little intelligence; for
> the incidents which give excellence to biography are of a volatile
> and evanescent kind, such as soon escape the memory, and are
> rarely transmitted by tradition.
>
> (*Rambler*, No. 60)

We can see from statements such as these why Johnson was an
admirer of Walton as a biographer and in his *Idler* essay he takes
the point to its logical conclusion: 'Those relations are therefore
commonly of most value in which the writer tells his own story',
he writes, a view which Boswell quotes at the beginning of *The
Life of Johnson*. Failing an autobiographer, the next best thing must
be a biographer who has personal knowledge of the subject, for
as Johnson put it on another occasion, 'Nobody can write the life
of a man, but those who have eat and drunk and lived in social

intercourse with him' (*Life of Johnson*, Everyman's Library edn., vol. I, p. 422). Boswell states his credentials on these grounds quite clearly on his opening page:

> As I had the honour and happiness of enjoying his friendship for upwards of twenty years; as I had the scheme of writing his life constantly in view; as he was well apprised of this circumstance, and from time to time obligingly satisfied my enquiries, by communicating to me the incidents of his early years . . . I flatter myself that few biographers have entered upon such a work as this with more advantages.
>
> (vol. I, pp. 5–6)

Boswell's *Life of Johnson* is one of those works whose very reputation has worked to its disadvantage. Appearing in 1791, it immediately superseded the work of Hawkins and Mrs Thrale, and the appearance of Croker's edition in 1831, reviewed by, most crucially, Macaulay and Carlyle, established both work and subject for succeeding generations in a particularly significant way. Macaulay's essay, tendentious and assertive, fixed the characters of both Johnson and Boswell in a way that made it unnecessary to read either the biography itself, or Johnson's own work. *The Life of Johnson*, in a very real sense, thus became established as a classic for people who need never have read a word of it, and while a further edition, that of Birkbeck Hill, published in 1887, both sustained the Johnson tradition and restored it to scholarly repute, the fact remains that Boswell's masterpiece is a work which everyone assumes to be part of their literary consciousness whether or not they can claim personal familiarity with it. Furthermore when we do read it I suspect that many of us, if we are honest, find it a daunting experience. We have Johnson's own authority for not reading books 'through', but an extended reading of *The Life of Johnson* is, by any standards, an arduous undertaking.

Length, of course, is part of the problem, but the greatest difficulty for the modern reader lies in the work's apparent lack of form. Bertrand H. Bronson, a distinguished modern Johnsonian,

has referred to 'Boswell's biographical art of disposition and pro-
portion, of anticipatory explanation and skilful highlighting, of
balance and perspective' (*Johnson Agonistes*, Berkeley and Los
Angeles, 1965, p. 175) and we do indeed know that Boswell
exercised considerable care over the organisation of his work.
While these qualities may be detected, however, they are not
immediately apparent as we read *The Life of Johnson*. Rather are
we struck by its seeming shapelessness: conversation follows
conversation, letters are compiled to fill in the gaps in Boswell's
personal experience of Johnson and, throughout, we have Boswell
at our shoulder, telling us what aspect of his hero each of his quoted
utterances is intended to illuminate. If there is an organising spirit
it lies in the pervasive presence of Johnson himself: in terms of
narrative structure we often find ourselves lost. A major reason
for this impression of formlessness is that *The Life of Johnson*
adopts the technique of the journal and it is, of course, the work
of the most assiduous journalist of English literary history. At the
time when Boswell was writing the distinction between biography
and journal was not as clear-cut as it is to us: journals, reminiscences, memoirs were the small-change of that literary sociability
of which Johnson's 'Club' was the apogee, and we have only to
consider the titles of the various accounts of Johnson himself to
take the point. Mrs Thrale's biography provides such an example:
*Anecdotes of the Late Samuel Johnson, Ll.D. during the last twenty
years of his life*. That word 'Anecdote' tells us that, in some ways,
biography has not advanced in sophistication since the age of
Aubrey.

In *The Life of Johnson*, however, Boswell applies his journalistic
technique with consistent seriousness. At various times he gives
us unashamed insights into his method, above all when he refers
to his habit of recording Johnson's conversation immediately *post
facto* with a view to using it as source-material for the work which,
throughout his years of acquaintance with Johnson, he had always
intended to write. Thus he is able to rebuke Mrs Thrale for her
own inaccuracies:

I have had occasion several times, in the course of this work, to point out the incorrectness of Mrs Thrale, as to particulars which consisted with my own knowledge. But indeed she has, in flippant terms enough, expressed her disapprobation of that anxious desire of authenticity which prompts a person who is to record conversations to write them down *at the moment*. Unquestionably, if they are to be recorded at all, the sooner it is done the better.

(vol. II, p. 554)

At an early stage in his acquaintance with Johnson Boswell tells us that he 'sat up all the night before recollecting and writing in my Journal what I thought worthy of preservation' (vol. I, p. 286), and it is clear that in rebuking Mrs Thrale Boswell was expressing his own commitment to his objectives

A direct consequence of Boswell's industry is our sense of the credibility of the events, and particularly the conversations, he records. *The Life of Johnson* is at its greatest when it re-enacts all those meetings at which 'we had good talk', and so anxious is Boswell to evoke the reality of the remembered moment that he repeatedly insists upon Johnson's physical pecularities, not simply for their own sake, but to recreate the scene which he records. Narrative effectively becomes drama, and Boswell at one point is brought to regret the limitations imposed upon him by cold print:

I cannot too frequently request of my readers, while they peruse my account of Johnson's conversation, to endeavour to keep in mind his deliberate and strong utterance. His mode of speaking was indeed very impressive; and I wish it could be preserved as music is written, according to the ingenious method of Mr Steele, who has shown how the recitation of Mr Garrick, and other eminent speakers, might be translated *in score*.

(vol. I, p. 534)

It might be added that Boswell not only gives an account of the play; in many cases he instigated the performance, as when, for example, he contrived the meetings between Paoli and Johnson and, more audaciously, Wilkes and Johnson, in order to see how Johnson would react. As Mrs Thrale remarked, 'he cared not what he provoked'. Thus Boswell can tell us, with unashamed candour that

> desirous of calling Johnson to talk, and exercise his wit, though I should myself be the object of it, I resolved to undertake the defence of convivial indulgence in wine, though he was not to-night in the most genial humour.

> (vol. I, p. 436)

The passage is typical of Boswell's behaviour towards Johnson: what we have in *The Life of Johnson* is not simply an accurate record of the events of an outstanding life, by someone who was there at the time, but a situation in which the writing of the biography and the events which it records are so closely inter-related that the biography itself can be said to have initiated its source-material. Intimacy between author and subject could scarcely have been taken further.

The high-points of *The Life of Johnson* are thus its recorded conversations, reinforced, as they are, by our strong sense of Johnson's physical presence. But the amount of time that Boswell actually spent in Johnson's company was comparatively short, and he is obliged to sustain his narrative with anecdotes from friends, with Johnson's own reminiscences, and with extensive correspondence. Boswell did not meet Johnson until the latter was fifty-four and he effectively devotes over three-quarters of his work to a period amounting to less than a third of Johnson's life. The direct use of what might be called secondary sources becomes in fact more extensive in the period with which Boswell deals in detail – the last twenty years of Johnson's life – than in the early pages of the book where Boswell moves in a prefatory manner through the time leading up to his first meeting Johnson. In spite of the recourse to such material, however, it is the great quality of *The Life of Johnson* that we never lose sight, not only of its subject, but also of its author, and one of the most interesting aspects of the book is the way in which it reflects their living relationship.

The mutual attraction – and it must not be forgotten that the attraction was mutual – of Boswell and Johnson is a phenomenon that has puzzled many commentators. The problem was resolved by Macaulay in his famous paradox to the effect that not only was the biography of a great man written by a fool but its very quality was directly attributable to that unlikely coincidence:

> That he (Boswell) was a coxcomb and a bore, weak, vain, pushing, curious, garrulous, was obvious to all who were acquainted with him ... In a happy hour he fastened himself upon Johnson. During twenty years the disciple continued to worship the master: the master continued to scold the disciple, to sneer at him, and to love him ... In this way were gathered the materials, out of which was afterwards constructed the most interesting biographical work in the world.

The judgement comes in Macaulay's second essay on Johnson, first published in 1856, and while it has now been substantially refuted, the problem it attempts to solve remains: how could two such apparently contradictory temperaments endure each other to the point where, even though they separated for long periods of time, they shared the relationship that resulted in *The Life of Johnson*? The question is not simply a matter of idle curiosity, for if we can understand something about the factors which sustained the relationship between Boswell and Johnson we can go some way towards understanding Boswell's capacity to convince us in his rendering of Johnson's inner life as well as his external circumstances, and this is an aspect which has wider implications for the way in which a biographer operates.

Initially hero-worship can explain Boswell's seeking-out of Johnson when he first came to London at the age of twenty-two. Boswell collected intellectual scalps: those of Hume, Wilkes, Rousseau and Voltaire were amongst the trophies which hung, or were to hang, from his belt. As Joseph Wood Krutch has pointed out, he did not necessarily admire what these people were 'because

one cannot really admire all those things at once. He admired each
of these men for being something' (*Samuel Johnson*, London, 1948,
p. 206). But with Johnson the case was rather different. The initial
impetus which guided Boswell to Johnson may have been similar
to that which guided him to his other heroes, but he did not
write their lives, nor did he ever intend to. He tells us that, prior
to meeting Johnson,

> I had for several years read his works with delight and instruction,
> and had the highest reverence for their author, which had grown
> up in my fancy with a kind of veneration, in which I supposed
> him to live in the immense metropolis of London.

> (vol. I, p. 238)

Knowing what we do of Boswell we may reasonably doubt his
capacity for receiving instruction – although he frequently expresses
his awareness of the need for it – but if the expression here is
one of a self-induced fantasy, it becomes clear from the passages
describing Boswell's first acquaintance with Johnson that while
the fantasy about him was to be qualified by the reality of his
presence, the reverence was ultimately to be confirmed. After
describing his reception by Johnson on his first visit to him Boswell
records his astonishment at his hero's physical appearance:

> His brown suit of clothes looked very rusty: he had a little
> shrivelled unpowdered wig, which was too small for his head;
> his shirt-neck and knees of his breeches were loose; his black
> worsted stockings ill drawn up; and he had a pair of unbuckled
> shoes by way of slippers. But all these slovenly particularities
> were forgotten the moment he began to talk.

> (vol. I, p. 245)

The final sentence is a key both to the fascination which Johnson
held for Boswell and which *The Life of Johnson* holds for us for, as
we have seen, it is Johnson's recorded talk which is the mainstay of
Boswell's account. What is perhaps important here though is the
way in which the detailed account of the reality which Boswell
discovered testifies to the fact that from that moment Johnson is

not to be simply another specimen to add to his collection of celebrities; from this point a work which had begun conventionally enough with details of the hero's early life borrowed from such sources as were available takes on a life of its own in which Boswell's 'veneration' for Johnson is substantiated by the instinctive naturalism of his method. For Boswell, Johnson never loses his heroic stature, but it is a stature of entirely human proportions, verified by a compound of lovingly recorded detail which effectively recreates the experiences which subject and author shared.

The Life of Johnson, then, is a record of a living relationship as well as of an individual life. It may seem, on face value, to be a one-sided relationship, but no relationship can be entirely so, and if we can ultimately only speculate about the source of Boswell's and Johnson's feelings for each other it is clear from *The Life of Johnson* that their mutual affection was powerful enough to remain unbroken until Johnson's death. The security of this relationship is perhaps the ultimate key to the power of Boswell's work for, realising that Johnson would always forgive as well as correct him, Boswell is free to be frank about his hero. We have seen how Boswell approached Johnson and what effect Johnson had upon him when they met: what is also revealed is the impact which Boswell had upon Johnson. Boswell himself expresses surprise at the nature of his reception:

> On reviewing, at the distance of many years, my journal of this period, I wonder how, at my first visit, I ventured to talk to him so freely, and that he bore it with so much indulgence.
>
> (vol. I, p. 247)

Many others have wondered at the same thing but, without self-importance, Boswell makes it clear that Johnson did more than tolerate him. He 'asked me why I did not come oftener to him' and, on being reminded of his initially discouraging reception of Boswell, Johnson, we are told replied '"Come to see me as often as you can. I shall be glad to see you."' A little later Boswell is preparing for a trip abroad and Johnson is genuinely moved: '"My dear

Boswell, I should be very unhappy at parting, did I think we were not to meet again."' (vol. I, p. 279).

Such instances of Johnson's feelings for Boswell are not thrust upon us, they appear in the natural course of the narrative, and in the letters of Johnson to Boswell that are quoted. Boswell is aware of the dangers involved – 'I hope my recording them will be ascribed to a better motive than to vanity', he writes of Johnson's comments – but it is one of the advantages of his naturalistic method that it can be. When Boswell leaves for the continent Johnson accompanies him to his embarkation point at Harwich, and we have one of the rarer reflective moments of *The Life of Johnson*:

> My revered friend walked down with me to the beach, where we embraced and parted with tenderness, and engaged to correspond by letters. I said, 'I hope, Sir, you will not forget me in my absence.' JOHNSON: 'Nay, Sir, it is more likely that you should forget me, than that I should forget you.' As the vessel put out to sea, I kept my eyes upon him for a considerable time, while he remained rolling his majestic frame in his usual manner; and at last I perceived him walk back into the town, and he disappeared.
>
> (vol. I, p. 293)

The closeness of Boswell and Johnson is clear from moments such as these, and perhaps particularly from their tour of the Western Highlands which, since it induced a separate account, is only briefly referred to in *The Life of Johnson*. It finds expression also in Boswell's insight into the pecularities of Johnson's character, most notably in his understanding of his melancholia. I have referred to speculation about the relationship between Boswell and Johnson, but it is not unreasonable to suggest that, in spite of all the apparent contradictions of character, the two figures had as much in common as they had in contrast. Boswell's frenetic activity, his absurd self-projection, his whoring and his drinking, like Johnson's self-professed lassitude, his carelessness of his appearance and his neurotic obsessions, may be seen as symptomatic of a deep-rooted mental disquietude which they both shared. In a remarkable metaphor Boswell describes Johnson's compulsive anxiety:

> His mind resembled the vast amphitheatre, the Colisæum at Rome. In the centre stood his judgement, which like a mighty gladiator, combated those apprehensions that, like the wild beasts of the *Arena*, were all around in cells, ready to be let upon him. After a conflict, he drives them back into their dens; but, not killing them, they were still assailing him.
>
> (vol. I, p. 378)

Reference to Johnson's mental disturbance is recurrent throughout Boswell's narrative and when Boswell comes to record 'the last time that I should enjoy in this world the conversation of a friend whom I so much respected' he reverts to it:

> Our conversation turned upon living in the country, which Johnson, whose melancholy mind required the dissipation of quick successive variety, had habituated himself to consider as a kind of mental imprisonment.
>
> (vol. II, p. 551)

Boswell too required 'the dissipation of quick successive variety', and it is an interesting, if obvious, paradox that *The Life of Johnson* effectively records both the unreason that threatened the mental processes of the intellectual giant of the Age of Reason and an authorial insight into it based upon personal experience. The interior life of Johnson, just as much as his public performance, is thus something which Boswell is able to convince us that he knew and understood.

Boswell's *Life of Johnson* thus fulfils Johnson's own requirements for biography: it records the domestic details of a life which affords moral instruction, while the proximity of author and subject are such as to ensure as nearly as possible the authenticity that, ideally, can only come from autobiography. Johnson's own greatest exercise in the form, his *Account of the Life of Mr Richard Savage* is on the face of it a complete contrast to Boswell's work: brief, ordered and austere in both form and expression, it employs an entirely different technique from that of Boswell. As always, however, Johnson's capacity for generalised abstraction is misleading and we can detect in the measured prose of *The Life of Savage* an element of personal feeling just as real as that which informs *The Life of Johnson*. Boswell, with perhaps an envy born of his own intimacy with Johnson, saw fit to disapprove of Savage, 'a man of whom it is difficult to speak impartially, without wondering that he was for some time the intimate companion of Johnson; for his character was marked by profligacy, insolence, and ingratitude' (vol. I, p. 94). So too was Boswell's; in *The Life of Savage*, as in *The Life of Johnson*, we have a subject-author relationship which is, on the face of it, surprising.

Ostensibly *The Life of Savage* is a variation on the favourite Johnsonian theme of the vanity of human wishes. The theme is announced on the opening page:

> That affluence and power, advantages extrinsic and adventitious, and therefore easily separable from those by whom they are possessed, should very often flatter the mind with expectations of felicity which they cannot give, raises no astonishment; but it seems rational to hope, that intellectual greatness should produce better effects...

> But this expectation, however plausible, has been very frequently disappointed ... volumes have been written only to enumerate the miseries of the learned, and relate their unhappy lives and untimely deaths.
>
> (*Samuel Johnson: Selected Writings*, ed. P. Cruttwell, Harmondsworth, 1968, p. 50)

The Life of Savage is to be another such volume, and its moral application is again stressed, if with rather different emphasis, at its conclusion:

This relation will not be wholly without its use, if those, who languish under any part of his sufferings, shall be enabled to fortify their patience, by reflecting that they feel only those afflictions from which the abilities of Savage did not exempt him; or if those, who, in confidence of superior capabilities or attainments, disregard the common maxims of life, shall be reminded, that nothing will supply the want of prudence; and that negligence and irregularity, long continued, will make knowledge useless, wit ridiculous, and genius contemptible.

(p. 133)

Here we have two moral generalisations which stand in rather odd contrast: those who suffer should reflect that even Savage, a man of great ability, was not exempted from the general lot of human suffering; alternatively anyone who prides himself on immunity from accepted standards of conduct should remember that nothing can be gained from indulgence in the human weaknesses which Savage embodied. These basic premises are reinforced at various stages in the course of Johnson's narrative by moral commentary arising from individual occurrences in Savage's career, and in this way *The Life of Savage* fulfils the requirement that biography should be instructive.

The overt moralisation is, as I have suggested, inconsistent, and furthermore it is compromised by the stance which Johnson takes towards his subject. In the first place Savage's misfortunes were so obviously the consequence of his own weaknesses that he scarcely serves as a satisfactory example of the inevitability of 'the miseries of the learned', and secondly Johnson is clearly so biassed in favour of Savage that he is unable to bring himself to affirm with any consistency the obvious moral lesson to be learned from his history: that 'negligence and irregularity', not to mention dissipation, parasitism, ill-temper and personal pride, are likely to reap their own reward. Johnson, in defence of Savage, extends his sympathy to the point where it becomes special pleading. When, for example, he writes:

> If his miseries were sometimes the consequences of his faults,
> he ought not yet to be wholly excluded from Compassion,
> because his faults were very often the effects of his misfortunes.
>
> (p. 77)

we respond to the generosity of feeling, but it is impossible to ignore
the fact that the details of Savage's career, even as it is presented
by Johnson, cannot justify the comment.

We know from Boswell that Johnson had 'eat and drunk' with
Savage, thus fulfilling another of his requirements of the biographer. We also know, however, that the two men can only have
known each other for a brief period of their lives: if we are to talk
in this case of intimacy between biographer and subject it is intimacy
of a very different kind from that which existed between Boswell
and Johnson. The stories which Johnson tells of Savage are all
in fact second-hand, and rest for their authenticity on an assumed
knowledge of Savage's character that stands in place of more formal
credentials. 'Whoever was acquainted with Mr. Savage', Johnson
will say *à propos* of a particular detail, or again, 'everyone that
knew Savage will readily believe', and go on to explain an incident
in terms invariably favourable to Savage himself. In this way we
are persuaded of an authority on the part of Johnson that is in
fact highly suspect. For example he accepts without question the
highly coloured, not to say improbable, account of Savage's
parentage which Savage himself had perpetrated, and he is similarly
uncritical about the reputed iniquity of Savage's supposed mother.
Elsewhere he seems hardly to consider the fact that the very fre-
quency of Savage's involvement in questions of honour must
ultimately tell against him. There is no remission of the details of
Savage's mis-spent life, but always the details are deployed in a
way which, while they scarcely do him credit, do much to turn
away any blame that the reader might feel. Finally, throughout
the work, Johnson seems to have abdicated his normal standards
of literary judgement, for Savage is always presented to us as a
writer of distinction, frustrated only by the demands of debt-

collectors and other injured parties. The judgement is one that neither Savage's contemporaries nor posterity have endorsed.

And yet, for all its obvious inadequacies as factual biography, *The Life of Savage* is infused with an honesty that exists independently of the requirements of verifiable fact. The question of Johnson's response to Savage involves an understanding not of Savage, but of Johnson, a far more complicated character. Such an investigation can scarcely be conducted here, but there are enough hints in *The Life of Savage* to show why Savage's career is presented as it is. Johnson knew Savage at a point in time when both were trying to establish themselves as literary figures in London and when they both suffered hardship as a consequence of their efforts. Savage, 'having no profession, became by necessity an author', Johnson tells us: he might indeed have said the same of himself. The opening paragraphs, from which I have already quoted, are a lament for the frustrations of the literary life and these were something to which Johnson, with rather more justice than Savage, could himself testify. Furthermore the incidentals of Savage's behaviour are often those of Johnson himself. 'He lodged as much by accident as he dined', we are told, and again, 'he ... would prolong his conversation till midnight, without considering that business might require his friend's application in the morning.' At a more serious level Johnson describes Savage's capacity for scholarship and commends his judgement 'both with regard to writings and man', while elsewhere he credits him with 'that inquisitiveness which must always be produced in a vigorous mind.' At moments such as these we feel that the feckless figure of Savage has been transformed into a projection of what Johnson might justifiably have felt about himself. Biography, like any other literary form, must ultimately be an expression of its author's own sensibility and we saw how, in Boswell's *Life of Johnson*, the degree of rapport between author and subject enabled Boswell to write with particular sympathy of those aspects of Johnson's character which found reflection in his own. In *The Life of Savage* the process reveals itself more comprehensively, and in this sense Johnson's biography of his friend becomes Johnsonian autobiography, effec-tively replacing the journal which, in defiance of his principles, he destroyed. The biographer is always likely to turn to a subject with whom he has instinctive sympathy, and in doing so, to reveal as much of himself as he does of his subject. In the matrix of relationships involving Boswell, Johnson and Savage it is Johnson, subject and author, who emerges in the fullest complexity.

4

Public legends: private lives

Opinion differs about the effect of Boswell on the biographers who followed him. Certainly *The Life of Johnson* achieved the kind of status that should have established once and for all the reputation not only of the work itself, but of biography as a literary form. Boswell's methodology might also have been expected to provide a model and indeed we can see reflections of it in most of the biographies of the nineteenth century: the dramatized conversation, the extended documentation and above all the massive comprehensiveness achieved by the nature of the relationship between subject and author are all aspects which, in various modified ways, can be traced in even the most inadequate biographical compilations of the next hundred years. And yet, with the memorable exception of Froude's four volume account of Carlyle (1882–4), it is difficult to think of another biography in English which reminds us of Boswell: we can identify the method, but the spirit is lost.

The reason for this is not difficult to find: it can be demonstrated quite simply by comparing the attitude of Boswell to that of Lockhart, the biographer of Scott. Lockhart was as close to Scott as was Boswell to Johnson, but in Lockhart's case that closeness, reinforced as it was by a domestic tie, was an ambiguous advantage. Referring to the temptation to '*Boswellize* Scott' Lockhart writes:

> To report conversations fairly, it is a necessary prerequisite that we should be completely familiar with all the interlocutors, and understand thoroughly all their minutest relations, and points of common knowledge, and common feeling with each

other. He who does not must be perpetually in danger ... For
this one reason, to say nothing of others, I consider no man
justified in journalizing what he sees and hears in a domestic
circle where he is not thoroughly at home; and I think there
are still higher and better reasons why he should not do so where
he is.

(*Life of Scott*, ch. 41)

Boswell often feels the need to justify his practice, but having done
so his instinct is to be frank. Lockhart replaces frankness by circumspection and the key phrases in his explanation indicate the nature
of that circumspection: 'perpetually in danger'; 'what he sees and
hears in a domestic circle'; 'still higher and better reasons'. Here,
in a work published in the first two years of Victoria's reign –
and examples can readily be found which pre-date it – we have
that deference to the code of domestic privacy which was to act
as a controlling restraint on the biographer's activities throughout
the Victorian period. As often as not biography was still to be
written by an intimate of the subject, but this was invariably for
a converse reason to that exemplified by *The Life of Johnson*: only
someone close to the subject could be trusted to exercise a proper
discretion about the personal details of a private life.

Leslie Stephen, himself an experienced biographer, wrote of
J. A. Froude that he was 'perhaps the most eminent man of letters
of his generation who has not become the victim of a biography.'
(*Studies of a Biographer*, London, 1898, vol. iii, p. 220.) The
omission was soon to be repaired, but the remark testifies to both
the proliferation of biography in the nineteenth century and the
widespread misgivings about its tendencies. The literary reviews
of the period reinforce this testimony: biographies are constantly
under review but the reviewer invariably feels called upon to discuss
the ethical issues raised by the form. Behind both the taste for
biography and the anxiety about it lies the commemorative impulse.
The Victorians did not hesitate to praise their famous men and
they praised them for the example that they set. Occasionally there

were anomalies: Southey's *Life of Nelson*, itself a pre-Victorian work, is cautious about Lady Hamilton, but tells us enough to make the nature of her relationship with Nelson clear to the most innocent reader, and yet the book became a classic of Victorian boys' litera- ture. The work is interesting in another way for it shows explicitly that much of Nelson's greatness lay in a capacity for not doing what he was told: Nelson is in fact a very ambivalent subject for exemplary biography. He was, however, already a legend by the time the work was written and legends are entitled to a certain freedom of conduct. Where more ordinary mortals are concerned the commemorative impulse and the claims of fact do not mix so easily and the result, as often as not, was what Richard Altick has referred to as 'studied discretion' (*Lives and Letters*, New York, 1969, p. 151) when the Victorians approached the private details of public lives. The conditions under which the Victorian biogra- pher worked bring to the forefront questions which have always been implicit in the form: what, if any, are the limits to be placed upon its tendency towards indecent as well as decent exposure of the privacy of the subject and, if limits are to be imposed, what effect does this have on the form itself?

In attempting to define the boundaries of permissible revelation in Victorian biography it is important to remember firstly that the most obvious taboos were not the only ones, and secondly that the existence of these prohibited areas was part of wider assump- tions about privacy which should not simply be seen in defensive terms. Sexual irregularities were obviously a subject for conceal- ment, but so too were drunkenness, mental instability and skeletons in the cupboards of the extended family. Religious doubts were rarely the subject of discussion: 'a friend's grave was no place for religious controversy' wrote Froude by way of approval of Carlyle's *Life of Sterling* (and perhaps disapproval of Archdeacon Hare's). Furthermore all these aspects were subsumed by the general and positively asserted belief that a man's relationship with his wife, his family and his God were not matters for public exposure. At the conclusion of *The Life of Charlotte Brontë* Mrs Gaskell writes, 'henceforward the sacred doors of home are closed upon her married life'. It was perhaps to Mrs Gaskell's advantage as a biographer that Charlotte Brontë's married life was so short. A similar discretion is deployed by Hallam Tennyson, whose *Memoir* of his father, published in 1897, tells us nothing of his relationship with Emily Sellwood, which endured for forty years. 'As a son,' he writes, 'I cannot allow myself full utterance about her whom I loved as perfect mother and "very woman of very woman."' The case is a telling one for it shows us that reticence was not simply a matter of concealing possible embarrassment: the happiest of marriages was entitled to its privacy. Stanley, in his *Life of Arnold*, in devoting a full chapter to Arnold's domestic felicity, in fact tells us rather more than we usually learn about the family life of a Victorian public figure. Furthermore, in the case of Hallam Tennyson's *Memoir*, it goes without saying that we get only the slightest hints of such matters as the distressing circumstances of his father's early life, or the temperamental instability which he largely, but never completely, outgrew. The intimacy between author and subject which had previously made for authenticity had, as we have seen, become a more ambivalent quality; in Victorian commemorative biography the closer the family tie the more securely the curtain of discretion was likely to be drawn.

What we are dealing with here is not a consciously applied censorship, however emphatic the biographers may have been about the boundaries of propriety, but a social and literary mode which would seem to be inimical to that curiosity about personality which we think of as one of the basic motives of the biographer. The question that we have to ask, therefore, is not so much what is the nature of the material which has been excluded, but whether that exclusion constricts the biographer to a point where it becomes impossible for him to practise his art. Now that we know, for example, that Kingsley decorated his letters to his future wife with erotic drawings does this substantially affect the view that we get of him from Mrs Kingsley's compilation of his life and letters? Superficially, of course, it must do, but the modern biographer

who concentrates on what a previous age has suppressed is as likely
to distort the evidence as his more cautious predecessors. Mrs
Kingsley's *Charles Kingsley* (1877) is a famous manifestation of
the memorial spirit but it remains the primary source of information
on its subject; furthermore more recent accounts of Kingsley would
suggest that even a skilled biographer, divested of family connections and in possession of all the facts, can really make little more
of his apparently aberrant behaviour than a diversionary idio-
syncrasy. With Tennyson the case is rather different, for we are
conscious throughout Hallam Tennyson's *Memoir* that one of the
most interesting of Victorian personalities is being hidden from
us by familial circumspection. Here is a case where reticence
clearly acts as a soporific and we are forced to ask whether
biography worthy of the name can be written under such cramping
conditions.

Biography which is inspired by motives of commemoration and
example inevitably involves the practitioner far more closely in the
manipulation of his material. By its nature it embodies a pre-
conceived attitude to its subject: the biographer will have clearly
in his mind the image of the subject which he wishes to project.
He cannot follow the policy which Lockhart professed in his *Life
of Scott* when he wrote 'it was my wish to let the character develop
itself'. In many cases this will imply obvious disadvantages: the
inadequate biographer – and it must be remembered that most
Victorian biographers were at best industrious amateurs – will
simply act as a censor, omitting from his account those details of
the subject's life which embarrass his pre-conceptions. Conversely,
however, the biographer's commitment to a particular view of his
subject can result in a shaping concept which will provide not
only motive but artistic coherence for the completed work. In two
of the biographies which have already been mentioned, Carlyle's
Life of Sterling (1851) and Mrs Gaskell's *Life of Charlotte Brontë*
(1857), we can see exactly how the author's firmly held view of
the subject's life operates to the advantage of the completed
work.

The factors surrounding the writing of Carlyle's *Life of Sterling* make it a particularly interesting case-history amongst Victorian biographies. The work is in fact a counter-biography, written because Carlyle, one of Sterling's literary executors, was dissatisfied with the official life produced by his co-executor, Archdeacon Hare. That work in itself is of rather more interest than its actual quality suggests for, unusually, it celebrates the life of a man whose career, in the author's eyes, was seriously flawed. John Sterling, a prominent Cambridge intellectual of whom great things were expected, failed, at least on the surface, to fulfil his potential. After taking orders somewhat later than might have been expected, he was actively involved in the ministry for only eight months. His intellectual history reveals endless self-searching, first through the medium of theological scholarship, and then through that of literary creation, but he achieved nothing of mark in either field. His mental development was paralleled by a tubercular complaint that rendered it necessary to be constantly searching for relief in appropriate climates, and which prevented him from ever settling to a fixed purpose. Sterling died in 1844 at the age of thirty-eight, an improbable hero for Victorian biography in that he had effectively achieved nothing in the eyes of the world.

In his account of Sterling's life, written as an introduction to a collection of his literary remains, Hare, a clergyman to whom Sterling had acted as curate during the short period of his ministry, makes no attempt to conceal his view of Sterling as a man who had, albeit excusably, failed. He gives extensive coverage to Sterling's interest in theology but apologises for him when that interest shifts to literary composition, explaining the development by 'his being compelled to abandon all projects of works requiring continuous thought and study' (*Essays and Tales by John Sterling, with a Memoir of his Life*, London, 1848, vol. I, p. cxxiii). Similarly, while Hare accepts Sterling's attribution of his resignation from his curacy to his illness, he feels bound to record the developing theological estrangement between Sterling and himself, of which his own sympathies allowed him only conventional understanding.

'He read Strauss's *Life of Jesus*,' Hare sadly reports, 'a book which a person can hardly read without being more or less hurt by it', (vol. I, p. cxxxiii). When he comes to sum up Hare has to explain why he has written of Sterling's 'errors':

> A bent tree is not to be drawn as a straight one; or the truth of history vanishes ... Hence the representation of my friend's life is unsatisfactory. By the omission of certain portions, it might easily have been made to appear more satisfactory: but then it would have been a lie: and every lie – O that people would believe it! is at best but a whited sepulchre.
>
> (vol. I, p. ccxxxi)

Hare's account of Sterling is now largely forgotten, and on the whole justifiably so, but its treatment of its hero is an interesting reminder of the dangers of generalisation about Victorian attitudes to biography in even the most apparently orthodox cases. But Hare's account would not be remembered at all were it not for the fact that it inspired Carlyle's *Life of Sterling*, and if we consider the two works together we can see how totally different views of the same subject can result from contrasting authorial stances. For Carlyle biography was a particularly significant form for it embodied a 'reality' which 'the whole class of Fictitious narratives' could only imitate. 'In some Boswell's *Life of Johnson*' he wrote 'how indelible and magically bright does many a little *Reality* dwell in our remembrance' (*Biography*, 1832). In his essay on Scott, effectively a review of Lockhart, Carlyle had inveighed against conventional biographic practice:

> How delicate, decent is English Biography, bless its mealy mouth! A Damocles' sword of *Respectability* hangs forever over the poor English Life-writer ... and reduces him to the verge of paralysis ... The English biographer has long felt that if in writing this Man's Biography, he wrote down anything that could by possibility offend any man, he had written wrong.

Carlyle, a theorist and practitioner of biography whose theories no one followed and whose practice no one emulated, would have none of Hare's view of Sterling as a man for whom apology had to be made. For him Sterling was not 'a vanquished *doubter*' but 'a victorious *doer*',

> An example to us all, not of lamed misery, helpless spiritual bewilderment and sprawling despair, or any kind of *drownage* in the foul welter of our so-called religious or other controversies and confusions; but of a swift and valiant vanquisher of all these; a noble asserter of himself, as worker and speaker, in spite of all these.
>
> (*Life of Sterling*, pt. I, ch. 1)

In this light Sterling's venture into the church is seen not as something which he failed to fulfil, but as a temporary aberration:

> To follow illusions till they burst and vanish is the lot of all new souls who, luckily or lucklessly, are left to their own choice in starting on this earth.
>
> (pt. II, ch. 2)

Seen in this light Sterling's release from his curacy is a positive step forward, furthermore the whole episode becomes representative of an issue of more than individual significance:

> It is in the history of such vehement, trenchant, far-shining and yet intrinsically light and volatile souls, missioned into this epoch to seek their way there, that we best see what a confused epoch it is.
>
> (ibid.)

Carlyle covers much the same ground as Hare but his radically different conception of Sterling always makes for crucial differences of interpretation. For Hare, for example, the influence of Coleridge upon Sterling had been that of the great advocate of a constitutional church: for Carlyle, Coleridge's ideas were a spurious diversion, injurious in their effect upon his friend – 'had there been no Coleridge, neither had this been' (pt. II, ch. 2). But it is not only in individual instances that we see the effect of Carlyle's view of Sterling: above all it provides a unifying factor in a beautifully structured work. Sterling is always before us, 'a young ardent soul looking ... with hope and joy ... into a world which was infinitely beautiful to him' (pt. I, ch. 4), and whatever vicissitudes he experiences these qualities remain. The various events of Sterling's life are used to illustrate this central concept, while his many travels – what Carlyle calls his 'peregrinities' – become an image of his spiritual journey through a world which Carlyle sees as hostile to a figure of his integrity.

In his presentation of Sterling Carlyle is primarily concerned with what he regards as his representative significance, in both a historical and a philosophical context. Sterling in fact takes on all the characteristics of the Teufelsdröckh of *Sartor Resartus*: 'Why,' Carlyle asks at one point, 'is a man so whipt by the furies ... if it is not even that he may seek some shrine, and there make expiation and find deliverance?' (pt. I, ch. 14). In this his purpose is more ambitious than that of Hare: the irony of Sterling's obscurity is that for Carlyle he has come to represent mankind. These large intentions, however, are firmly underpinned by close reference to the factual realities of Sterling's career, of which Carlyle gives a rather fuller account than his predecessor, and above all by the sympathetic detail with which Carlyle records his own acquaintance with Sterling. Of one of their meetings he writes:

> We went accordingly together; walking rapidly, as was Sterling's wont, and no doubt talking extensively. It probably was in the end of February: I can remember leafless hedges, gray driving clouds; – procession of boarding-school girls in some quiet part of the route.
>
> (pt. II, ch. 4)

Here the rhetorical projection of Sterling that dominates the life gives way to the authenticity of recollected detail. Believing the detail, we are more prepared to respond to the controlling design of the work as a whole.

The case of Sterling shows the difference between a compilation of biographical data, albeit written with a particular bias, and a projection of a consistently realised personality. It reminds us too that any biography will depend upon the inevitably partial viewpoint of its author. Both Hare and Carlyle make extensive use of Sterling's letters to document their point of view: if the content of the letters quoted by Hare tends to support his view of Sterling as a man deeply committed to his theological investigations Carlyle is equally able to support his case with letters of which the style and the sentiments might easily be his own. Both biographies originated in personal friendship and they testify to the way in which different aspects of personality must have revealed themselves in the different relationships. Finally both biographies extract full effect from the end of Sterling's life when, as Hare records 'within two hours he found himself deprived both of his mother and of his wife', (p. ccvi) following which he faces his last year in the knowledge of his oncoming death. In Hare, in particular, the Victorian tendency to exploit the impact of death is indulged: it is there too, in Carlyle, but rendered in such a way as to provide a genuinely tragic perspective to his account, and this too is a consequence of the successful substantiation of his conception of Sterling throughout the book.

Hare and Carlyle commemorated the life of a man who had promised to become a public figure, but had lapsed into obscurity. They had also been dealing with a figure whose life had given little cause, apart perhaps from its religious trials, for the exercise of discretion. Its only spectacular event had been Sterling's involvement with a group of Spanish revolutionaries, an incident which both Hare and Carlyle feel free to report. In Mrs Gaskell's *Life of Charlotte Brontë*, my other example of Victorian biography which is beneficially influenced by its author's convictions, these situations are reversed. Charlotte Brontë was a private figure whose novels had made her a public property, while many of the events not only of her own life but of the lives of those around her were potentially dangerous to a biographer in Mrs Gaskell's situation.

Throughout *The Life of Charlotte Brontë*, and in the letters which Mrs Gaskell wrote while working on the book, there is constant reference to the strain imposed upon her by the requirements of delicacy. At the same time however, Mrs Gaskell becomes increasingly committed to her view of Charlotte Brontë; as she wrote to her publisher:

> I *really* think ... that leaving all authorship on one side, her character as a woman was unusual to the point of being unique ... Everything she did, and everything she said and wrote, bore the impress of this remarkable character.
>
> (*The Letters of Mrs Gaskell*, ed. J. A. V. Chapple
> and Arthur Pollard, Manchester, 1966, p. 417)

What is particularly interesting in the context of this discussion is the extent to which Mrs Gaskell allowed herself to be influenced on matters of discretion by the way in which she wanted to portray her heroine. Where revelation might have conflicted with her shaping design she was reticent: where it confirmed it she relaxed. The result is that whereas her contemporaries criticised her (and to the point where the work had to be withdrawn and revised) for what she included, modern commentators have tended to emphasise what she left out.

Mrs Gaskell was originally commissioned to write *The Life of Charlotte Brontë* as a consequence of the public interest which Charlotte Brontë's literary career had aroused. Her own interest in her heroine however was of a more personal kind: the two authoresses had met and communicated in the friendliest of terms for the last four years of Charlotte Brontë's life. Thus it is that Mrs Gaskell's major concern is with the representation of a friend whom she admired, rather than a public figure, or as she herself put it, 'Charlotte Brontë the woman' rather than 'Currer Bell, the author'. Furthermore the view of her friend which she came to hold with increasing firmness as she worked on the project was of an intensely sensitive figure who always sacrificed personal inclination to the higher call of duty. In the penultimate paragraph of *The Life of Charlotte Brontë* she quotes, as an epitaph, the verdict of Charlotte Brontë's friend, Mary Taylor:

> She thought much of her duty, and had loftier and clearer notions of it than most people, and held fast to them with more success. It was done, it seems to me, with much more difficulty than people have of stronger nerves, and better fortunes. All her life was but labour and pain; and she never threw down the burden for the sake of present pleasure.
>
> (*The Life of Charlotte Brontë*, Penguin edn., p. 526)

These words describe exactly the character of Charlotte Brontë as it is rendered by Mrs Gaskell but they also suggest a delicate problem of balance for the biographer. Virtue, to be worth anything, must be seen to be tested, and Charlotte's adherence to her duty must be seen to cost her a great deal. On the other hand the tension involved in her situation must never be shown to be too great, lest it should appear that she followed her duty only unwillingly. What Mrs Gaskell has therefore to do is show all those incidents and aspects of Charlotte Brontë's situation that demonstrate her ideal of duty, and at the same time emphasise those aspects of her life which caused her to suffer. What she has to hold in check is the suggestion that Charlotte Brontë might in any way have shown the kind of emotional and intellectual rebelliousness of, for example, her own fictional creations. It is these factors which dictate Mrs Gaskell's attitude to her source-material, so much of which raised questions of elementary propriety.

The clearest instance of the way in which Mrs Gaskell's conception of Charlotte Brontë affected her use of source-material comes, as is well-known, in her treatment of the issue of Charlotte Brontë's relationship with her Brussels tutor, Constantin Heger. As it appears in *The Life of Charlotte Brontë* this is simply a functional relationship, exciting at best in Charlotte feelings of respect for a distinguished teacher. Charlotte Brontë's letters to Heger, however, of which it is now reasonable to assume that Mrs Gaskell saw at least a substantial part, suggest a far more intense emotional involvement on her part. In sup-pressing this material Mrs Gaskell was obviously taking the only course open to her but the issue is more complex than a simple covering-up of what might hint at impropriety. In fact the Heger letters, while emotionally overwrought, carry little to suggest an improper attachment. What they do indicate is that Charlotte Brontë's self-denial at Haworth was often unwillingly achieved, and that her obsession with Heger was the expression of her sense, if only in fantasy, of an alternative existence. Mrs Gaskell does indeed record the mental suffering that was a consequence of Charlotte Brontë's commitment to Haworth, but scarcely with the intensity suggested by Charlotte's language to Heger in her letters. The suppression of this material is thus more than a matter of propriety, although it was certainly that; it glosses over an aspect of Charlotte Brontë's experience that did not entirely accord with Mrs Gaskell's overall picture.

By way of contrast, Mrs Gaskell's handling of issues which emphasise the extent of Charlotte Brontë's suffering shows little regard for conventional discretion. She has only formal com-punction about revealing the iniquities of Branwell Brontë and the idiosyncracies of his father, both obvious intrusions of family privacy, and she exposed herself to the threat of legal action both by identifying Branwell Brontë's 'seducer' and by her account of the Clergy Daughters' School. In all these instances Mrs Gaskell's determination to substantiate her view of Charlotte Brontë led her to ignore normal standards of reticence: indeed, for the sake of emphasis, she was prepared to exaggerate this inflammatory material.

The commemorative spirit, therefore, is not always the encum-brance that detractors of Victorian biography would have us believe. To suggest, as does Sir Harold Nicolson, that 'Hagiography ... returned in stately triumph with Dean Stanley's *Life of Arnold*, and continued throughout the century, culminating in such works as Mr Horton's study of Tennyson in the "Saintly Lives" series of Messrs. Dent' (*The Development of English Biography*, London,

1927, pp. 126–7) is grossly to misrepresent both a major work and the Victorian achievement in general. The best commemorative biography capitalizes on its commitment to its subject, offering a personal viewpoint that no clinical analysis could obtain. There is perhaps one further characteristic that should be mentioned. Of its nature, commemorative biography tends to instigate legend. In spite of the legal quibbles of her detractors, Mrs Gaskell's image of Charlotte Brontë was seized upon by less discriminating enthusiasts: the Brontë industry had begun. Similarly the Arnold cult transformed the hero of Stanley's *Life* to a figure whom his disciples would scarcely have recognized and facilitated Lytton Strachey's derision. But the biographer can scarcely be held responsible for such by-products of his success. When we strip away the accretions of legend and return to the original we are often surprised to find that in spite of the distinct authorial point of view there is little that we can fault in the essentials of the interpretation. Our adjustments of detail are effectively minor corrections in the light of the biographer's knowledge of his subject and his belief in his ideal.

5

Truth of fact and truth of fiction

Until the beginning of this century there had been little tendency
to regard biography as an art-form in its own right. Such discussion of the genre as there had been had involved questions either
of morality or of practice, and the motivation of the biographer
had been seen primarily as a functional one, whether to record,
to praise, or to instruct. But, acting in the light of the biographies
of Lytton Strachey, and in particular of his appeal to the artistic
consciousness in the preface to *Eminent Victorians*, a number
of writers in the earlier part of this century, most notably Virginia
Woolf, but also figures like Sir Harold Nicolson and André
Maurois, began to talk of biography as an art, with a tradition and
requirements of its own. All of these writers had connections, albeit
sometimes tenuous, with Bloomsbury, and it was Strachey whom
they saw as having reclaimed biography from the province of the
literary drudge. 'A book by Trevelyan or by Lockhart ... is above
all things a document; a book by Mr Strachey is above all things
a work of art,' wrote André Maurois (*Aspects of Biography*,
London, 1929, p. 9), while for Sir Harold Nicolson the entertain-
ment value of *Eminent Victorians* concealed the profoundest intellectual qualities:

> Everybody was delighted and amused, but when they had
> recovered from their amusement they realised that behind it all
> lay something far more serious and important – a fervent belief,
> for instance, in intellectual honesty; and an almost revivalist
> dislike of the second-hand, the complacent, or the conventional;

a derisive contempt for emotional opinions; a calm conviction that thought and reason are in fact the most important elements in human nature; a respect ultimately for man's unconquerable mind. It is in directions such as these that Mr. Strachey has moulded the spirit of the age.

(*The Development of English Biography*, p. 150)

Edmund Gosse's astringent account of his father in *Father and Son*, published in 1907, and thus pre-dating *Eminent Victorians* by over a decade, together with a detected irony in Froude's *Carlyle*, were seen as precursors of this new biographical spirit, but it was Strachey who was seen as the founder of the 'New Biography' – the term is Virginia Woolf's – and while we may question the validity of a judgement which presents Strachey as a model of the rational temper it cannot be denied that the kind of biography he wrote, and the discussion to which it gave rise, are symptomatic of changes in attitude in the mood and priorities of twentieth-century biographers.

An exposition of the new critical attitude to biography is to be found in two essays by Virginia Woolf, 'The Art of Biography' and 'The New Biography' (both reprinted in *Virginia Woolf: Collected Essays*, ed. Leonard Woolf, London, 1967, vol. IV). In 'The Art of Biography' Virginia Woolf argues that 'towards the end of the nineteenth century ... for reasons not easy to discover, widows became broader-minded, the public keener-sighted; the effigy no longer carried conviction or satisfied curiosity. The biographer certainly won a measure of freedom.' The chief exponent of that freedom, she argues, was Strachey, who set a pattern for a biographer who 'is no longer the serious and sympathetic companion' but who, 'whether friend or enemy, admiring or critical ... is an equal (who) preserves his freedom and his right to independent judgement' ('The New Biography'). The immediate attraction of Stracheyan biography, then, lies in its rejection of the moralistic constraints placed upon it by its predecessors and in particular in the spirit of detachment – 'the lack of pose, humbug, solemnity' – in which the biographer conducts his activities. This shift of authorial stance, however, embraces a more fundamental change in the biographer's attitude. The intellectual freedom reflects a shift of concern from the externals of individual achievement to the less easily definable but more vital area of the nature of individual personality, and thus, 'Many of the old chapter headings – life at college, marriage, career – are shown to be very arbitrary and artificial distinctions. The real current of the hero's existence took, very likely, a different course' ('The Art of Biography').

'The real current of the hero's existence' – this is what the biographer has to record, and the shift of priorities presents him with problems which only the artist, as distinct from the compiler of biographical records, will be able to solve. Of the biographers of the past, Virginia Woolf tells us in 'The New Biography', only Boswell in isolated moments managed to recreate 'personality' as distinct from a life which consists of 'actions' and 'works'. Emphasis on the workings of the personality, of course, is something that we find throughout Virginia Woolf's work: all of her major novels, for example, are attempts to record (not to explain) personality in action, and indeed, in the light of the activities of the founders of modern psychology, the issue is one which concerned novelists and biographers alike at this time. The difficulties for the biographer – and for the novelist – are considerable for it is of the nature of personality that it is inconsistent, unpredictable and, as Virginia Woolf says, 'of rainbow-like intangibility'. In *Orlando*, published shortly after 'The New Biography' in 1928, Virginia Woolf produced a fantasy-biography in which she parodied the activities of the traditional biographer, and taunted him with his inability to capture the essentials of the life which he recorded. Setting out to record the life of her hero Orlando, a figure incidentally who lives for four hundred years during the course of which he changes his sex, she writes:

Directly we glance at eyes and forehead, we have to admit a

thousand disagreeables which it is the aim of every good biographer to ignore. Sights disturbed him, like that of his mother, a very beautiful lady in green walking out to feed the peacocks … sights exalted him … the birds and the trees … the evening sky, the homing rooks … all these sights, and the garden sounds too, the hammer beating and the wood chopping, began that riot and confusion of the passions and emotions which every good biographer detests.

(Penguin edn., p. 11)

The inescapable characteristics of personality, its irrationality and its variety, are seen here as a direct challenge to the orderly proceedings of the biographical method.

For Virginia Woolf the biographer, like the novelist, is thus faced with the task of making order out of chaos. He must be aware, in the first place, that 'man himself, the pith and essence of his character, shows itself to the observant eye in the tone of a voice, the turn of a head, some little phrase or anecdote picked up in passing.' Furthermore, while his source-material must inevitably be factual, the biographer has to deploy the techniques of the novelist, and here indeed lies his greatest difficulty:

Truth of fact and truth of fiction are incompatible; yet he is more than ever urged to combine them. For it would seem that the life which is increasingly real to us is the fictitious life; it dwells in the personality rather than in the act. Each of us is more Hamlet, Prince of Denmark, than he is John Smith of the Corn Exchange. Thus, the biographer's imagination is always being stimulated to use the novelist's art of arrangement, suggestion, dramatic effect to expand the private life. Yet if he carries the use of fiction too far, so that he disregards the truth, or can only introduce it with incongruity, he loses both worlds; he has neither the freedom of fiction nor the substance of fact.

('The New Biography')

In the same essay she tells us that 'in order that the light of personality may shine through, facts must be manipulated; others shaded; yet in the process they must never lose their integrity.' The biographer 'chooses; he synthesises; in short he has ceased to be the chronicler; he has become the artist.'

Ideally then, for Virginia Woolf, choice and synthesis, accompanied by a sense of form – 'shaping the whole,' as she says 'so that we perceive the outline' ('The Art of Biography') – will reveal the ultimate truth about the personality of the subject. But as she is so clearly aware, the danger is that the truth of fiction will distort the truth of fact, and if we revert to those biographies by Strachey which prompted her theorizing it is easy to see how serious this distortion can become. Consider, for example, the following passage from Strachey's description of Thomas Arnold in *Eminent Victorians*:

> His outward appearance was the index of his inward character, everything about him denoted energy, earnestness, and the best intentions. His legs, perhaps, were shorter than they should have been; but the sturdy athletic frame, especially when it was swathed (as it usually was) in the flowing robes of a Doctor of Divinity, was full of an imposing vigour ... His eyes were bright and large; they were also obviously honest. And yet – why was it? Was it in the lines of the mouth or the frown on the forehead? – it was hard to say, but it was unmistakeable – there was a slightly puzzled look on the face of Dr. Arnold.
>
> (Penguin edn., p. 165)

Here Strachey does exactly what Virginia Woolf recommends, extracting 'the pith and essence' of Arnold's character from a set of observational details. But the total effect is not one of the distillation of essentials, but of carefully contrived caricature. Quite apart from the heavily ironic tone it is clear that Strachey here is closer to fiction than even the most liberal interpretation of the facts would allow. It has been disputed, as it happens, that Arnold's legs were noticeably short – or does the 'should have been' imply that Strachey required longer legs of Arnold than he might have done of other men? Strachey heads his short list of bibliographical sources at the conclusion of his essay with Stanley's *Life of Arnold* but there is little in Stanley to suggest either the excessive muscularity or the rhetorical speculations about the 'lines of the mouth or the frown on the forehead'. Furthermore if we compare Strachey's overall presentation of Arnold with that given by Stanley we find that an important figure not only of English educational life, but of church and national politics at a critical time in their development, has been reduced to the parody figure of Strachey's selective imagination. Even on the issue of personality it might be said that Stanley has the edge for it is he who records the paradoxes of Arnold's character – his distaste for his Rugby environment, for example, at the very time when he was becoming 'Arnold of Rugby' and his capacity, as A. O. J. Cockshut has put it, for combining 'the loftiest aims with the earthiest realism' (*Truth to Life*, London, 1974, p. 94). In doing so he reveals, even if unconsciously, rather greater subtlety than we find in Strachey's more consciously artistic essay.

It might, of course, be argued that Strachey's essay on Arnold, which anyway is the shortest of the four studies that compose *Eminent Victorians*, is a special case. Virginia Woolf herself referred to the element of 'the over-emphasis and the foreshortening of caricatures' in *Eminent Victorians* ('The Art of Biography') and it is clear that Strachey saw Arnold through the double-filter of the Arnold legend, in which *Tom Brown's Schooldays* played as great a part as Stanley's *Life of Arnold*, and his own distasteful experiences of a Victorian public school: the result is a cynical reworking of the Arnold of Hughes's fiction supported by selective treatment of Stanley's facts. But the investment of individual moments with a comprehensive significance is bound to embody the kind of dangers revealed in Strachey's Arnold essay: to take another example, Arthur Hugh Clough has still hardly recovered from Strachey's detail of his wrapping up brown-paper parcels in the service of Florence Nightingale. Strachey's longer biographies, *Queen Victoria* and *Elizabeth and Essex*, are perhaps fairer tests of this kind of biographic method. In *Elizabeth and Essex* Strachey was in a sense freer to indulge in the imaginative approach since, where the actual life of his major subject, Queen Elizabeth, is concerned, the remoteness of the period and the unreliability of such factual evidence as can be gathered should have liberated his impulse towards a predominantly artistic recreation. Even the imaginative biographer, however, cannot construct a life without the relevant facts to choose from and, as Virginia Woolf herself observed, Strachey's experiment in this instance falls awkwardly between the stools of fact and fantasy. And in *Queen Victoria*, where Strachey does deploy a considerable range of factual evidence, and where it could be most genuinely claimed that he has achieved the realisation of personality, it has still to be admitted that this realisation is his own artefact, in its own way as reductive of the 'riot and confusion' of an individual life as any impersonal account of its public events might be. The 'New Biography', in fact, failed to live up to its advocates' claims in terms not only of the substance of its achievements but also of its capacity to revolutionise the form. As a novelist Virginia Woolf had recourse to stream of consciousness to resolve the problems posed by personality: as a biographer, apart from the special case of her account of Roger Fry, she restricted herself on the one hand, like many of her contemporaries, to occasional essays which stand in relation to biography as the vignette does to the full-length portrait, and on the other to *Orlando*, entirely the construct of her own fantasy, and to *Flush*, the biography of Elizabeth Barrett Browning's dog.

The most substantial advances in modern biography would seem to have been made, apparently in defiance of the principles laid down by Strachey's admirers, by the scholars rather than the artists. Virginia Woolf remarked that 'the first and most visible sign' of the change which came over biography at the beginning of this century was 'the difference in size':

In the first twenty years of the new century biographies must have lost half their weight. Mr. Strachey compressed four stout

Victorians into one slim volume; M. Maurois boiled the usual
two volumes of a Shelley life into one little book the size of
a novel.

('The New Biography')

It is one of the minor ironies of the genre that Strachey himself
has been celebrated by Michael Holroyd in one of the most massive
biographies of the modern period, a book in fact which its author
divided into separate parts when it came to be reprinted. Size is
indeed as characteristic of what, for the sake of generalised defini-
tion, I will call the 'research biography' as it is of Strachey's own
work.

The research biographer inevitably takes as his standard 'truth
of fact'. J. L. Clifford, the biographer of Johnson and Mrs Thrale,
has given an account of his own activities in this field in *From
Puzzles to Portraits* (London, 1970). In a chapter entitled 'Testing
authenticity' he makes it clear that in his view the biographer has
a scholarly duty to check even the most peripheral anecdote for,
'the biographer's duty is to reproduce the truth as closely as he
humanly can' (p. 81). Clifford describes how the search for material
takes place not only in the library but, as it were, in the field,
where the scholar must follow up every possible hint of information.
He sees the biographer as a detective, and

> as every detective knows, clues keep turning up which are quite
> unconnected with the main problem but which eventually lead
> to others equally important. A stray remark or a seemingly futile
> suggestion may start one off on a completely new trail. And the
> scholar soon learns that it is never safe to ignore any possible
> lead.

(ibid., p. 41)

Clifford's own researches lead him to the most remote places in
search of primary sources: seeking a detail about Johnson's financial
situation he finds himself at work in the vaults of a London bank
on 'a number of huge dusty ledgers, very thick and very heavy'
from which he eventually extracts material for 'one possible sen-

tence for my book'. It would be difficult to invent a more vivid dramatization of the research method, and yet throughout Clifford's account one gets the sense, not of labour, but of the excitement of the quest. Furthermore Clifford himself is quick to acknowledge that the accumulation of facts is only a preliminary exercise: what ultimately will matter is what happens when, as Leon Edel, another modern biographer who has described his own experiences puts it, 'the biographer is called upon to impose logic and coherence upon the heterogeneous mass of facts he has assembled, recognizing that in the life he is pursuing they seemed quite arbitrary and, on occasion, illogical' (*Literary Biography*, London, 1957, p. 45).

Edel describes this imposition of coherence as the 'critical' function of the biographer but in his emphasis on the biographer's shaping of apparently arbitrary material he comes very close to the artistic role defined by Virginia Woolf when she talked of the need for synthesis and choice, while the process is motivated by a similar need to create that form in the literary work which will project the personality of the subject. A. J. A. Symons in *The Quest for Corvo* (London, 1934) adopted the ingenious method of writing a biography of Corvo by means of describing his own investigations into his career rather than the career itself. Fascinated by a chance reading of Corvo's novel, *Hadrian VII*, he is determined to discover all he can about 'how Rolfe's (Corvo's) masterpiece came to be written, and what manner of man its author was.' Symons, like Clifford, follows every possible lead but he argues that where information is scanty his sense of the subject's personality will allow him to work by inference. Lacking information about Corvo's childhood, he passes on, for 'it is possible to reason backwards as well as forward, to infer the child from the man and I proposed to do so.' (p. 50). Symons was in fact much influenced by Bloomsbury biographers: in *The Quest for Corvo* he explains that his book embodies the principles he had expressed in his earlier essay, 'Tradition in Biography', in which he had adopted a stance very similar to that of Virginia Woolf, arguing that 'to omit is as important as to mention' and that 'the true battle (i.e. for the potential biographer) is between the unguided instinct and self-consciousness and I am on the side of self-consciousness ('Tradition in Biography', reprinted in *Essays and Biographies by A. J. A. Symons*, ed. Julian Symons, London, 1969, pp. 1–9).

For Edel, who himself pays frequent tribute to Virginia Woolf, the process of achieving that coherence and form which will express what he calls 'the essence of a life' is one of organisation rather than of selection and omission. He is particularly conscious of the deceptive nature of 'mechanical time': 'attach a biography to mechanical time and you will run the risk of having a mechanical biography' (*Literary Biography*, p. 99). The significance of the separate events of an individual life, he argues, will vary, and will ultimately depend upon a net-work of inter-relationships and emphases that operate independently of chronological sequence. Edel cites an example from his own biography of Henry James where he deals with James's acquaintance with Emerson. James met Emerson in 1870 and in 1872, he attended his funeral in 1883 and he wrote about him in 1887. Edel tells us that he made a positive decision to telescope events spanning seventeen years into one substantial scene, 'weaving backward and forward in time, and even dipping into the future', and he insists that he does this 'in violation of all chronology, dealing with my subject's relation to Emerson at the most meaningful moment that I can find' (ibid., pp. 101–3). The priority is one which Edel adopts throughout the biography: there is a particularly illuminating instance, to which he himself calls attention, at the opening of the fourth volume. Here, having concentrated all his attention at the conclusion of the previous volume on the death in Venice of James's friend Constance Fenimore Woolson, Edel reverts to a series of earlier events unconnected with that incident, but vital to his story, before continuing his narrative. While adopting an overall chronological structure, assigning a period of time to each of his five volumes, Edel is all the time conscious of those aspects of his subject-matter which cannot be tied to a linear concept of time and which appear like recurrent themes in his account of James's career. The result is a kind of counterpoint in which chronology and theme interact.

Edel's acknowledgement of chronology equates to Virginia Woolf's 'truth of fact'; his consciousness of the demands made upon the biographer by such aspects as theme, coherence and form to her 'truth of fiction'. Not all research biographers have followed his example: Edward Nehls, for example, in his aptly titled *D. H. Lawrence: A Composite Biography*, (1957) deliberately accumulates all the evidence available to him and places it in chronological order, allowing it simply to speak for itself, and using wherever possible the actual words in which it had been presented. Even here though Nehls himself is always present as the compiler and arranger: there are respectable fictional precedents for the course which he adopts.

There are, of course, more obvious and perhaps less acceptable ways in which the biographer will usurp the role of the novelist than any of those mentioned so far. It is a major temptation, for example, in the effort to achieve authenticity to substitute the persuasive hypothesis for the verifiable fact. An instance from the most recent of the many biographies of Charlotte Brontë will illustrate the point. In an account of the reception by an unfortunate suitor of the rejection of his proposal to Charlotte we are told, 'Henry opened the letter, sighed, and made another diary entry' (Margot Peters, *Unquiet Soul*, London, 1975, p. 64). We can verify the letter, and the diary entry, but is it just an excess of academic purism that makes us object that we have no evidence that Henry sighed? I suspect not, for the problem here is that in an intermingling of fact and invention, however much the latter is sustained by probability, the reader must lose confidence in the reliability of the author. The point can be emphasised by reverting to Edel who, after describing Constance Woolson's death, reflects that James was to write a novel about a death in Venice which he called *The Wings of the Dove*. This induces the observation that at this time James may have read the sixty-eighth psalm, from which his title is taken. But Edel maintains his biographical integrity by making it perfectly clear that this is only hypothesis: the reader thus knows exactly where he stands. There are indeed a whole class of works constructed entirely on the hypothetical basis – books like Michael Foot's *The Pen and the Sword* which deals with the political career of Swift, and Irving Stone's popular accounts of Van Gogh, *Lust for Life*, and Michaelangelo, *The Agony and the Ecstasy*. These are effectively a separate form, however, closer in many ways to the historical novel than to biography as such, and there are obvious dangers in deploying their techniques in the service of a more serious biographical purpose.

The research biographer is thus not so different in the nature of his activities from the theorists of the earlier part of this century as external appearances would suggest. Like them, he operates in the light of that irreversible change in our attitudes towards human personality of which the pioneering psychologists were as much symptom as cause. He may indeed call on the skills of the psychologist in his efforts to interpret the life of his subject: whether or not he does so specifically his practise is inevitably analogous to that of the psychologist since for both men the external events of a human life are only the symbols by which they attempt to comprehend its inner reality. The biographer will overlap with the historian on the one hand and with the novelist on the other, but he will never supplant them for historian, novelist and biographer each have their own motivation, their own methods and their own ends. What has been accomplished for biography in this century is a more consistently serious attitude towards the literary problems raised by the genre itself.

Bibliography

The study of biography as a literary form has produced a relatively small number of full-scale studies and a very large number of shorter essays and articles, often by active practitioners. In the very selective list which follows I have concentrated on the former and referred only to the latter where they seem to me to be of particular interest or importance. Items marked with an asterisk themselves contain substantial bibliographies which will enable the reader to supplement these suggestions as extensively as he may wish.

The first modern attempt to cover the history of biography is W. H. Dunn, *English Biography*, London, 1916. Harold Nicolson, *The Development of English Biography*, London, 1927, covers much the same ground, but with a critical perspective heavily influenced by Bloomsbury. Edgar Johnson, *One Mighty Torrent: the Drama of Biography*, New York, 1937, is always stimulating, but concentrates on the biographical subjects as much as on matters of form. The two most complete studies of the subject are J. A. Garraty, *The Nature of Biography*, New York, 1957*, a comprehensive study of developments from classical literature onwards, and R. D. Altick, *Lives and Letters*, New York, 1969*, which deals primarily with English and American biography from Boswell and Johnson to the present day. Altick's is easily the most stimulating of these studies: it is splendidly, if often provocatively, informative, particularly on the nineteenth century. Selected passages of criticism and theory written between 1560 and 1960 are anthologised in J. L. Clifford, *Biography as an Art*, London, 1962*.

On individual periods of literary history, D. A. Stauffer, *English*

Biography before 1700, Cambridge, Mass., 1930, and, by the same author, *The Art of Biography in Eighteenth Century England*, Princeton, 1941, are standard works of scholarship, the first of which may be usefully supplemented by two anthologies, D. Nichol Smith, *Characters of the Seventeenth Century*, Oxford, 1918, and V. de S. Pinto, *English Biography in the Seventeenth Century*, London, 1951. The eighteenth century is also covered by P. B. Daghlian, ed., *Essays in Eighteenth Century Biography*, Bloomington, Indiana, 1968, while John Butt, *Biography in the Hands of Walton, Johnson and Boswell*, Los Angeles, 1966, devotes itself specifically to these major figures. This bibliography will not normally concern itself with individual authors, but O. M. Brock, Jr., and R. Kelley, *The Early Biographies of Samuel Johnson*, Iowa City, 1974 and *Samuel Johnson's Early Biographies*, Iowa City, 1971, the former an anthology and the latter a descriptive account, are of interest in terms of eighteenth century biographical practice generally. J. W. Reed, Jr., *English Biography in the Early Nineteenth Century*, New Haven and London, 1966, deals usefully with an important period of transition which I am conscious of not having dealt with adequately in this study. Apart from Altick's study already mentioned, Victorian biography has received surprisingly little detailed attention: A. O. J. Cockshut, *Truth to Life*, London, 1974, is written in awareness of the deficiency, and with very real feeling for the form and the period, but these qualities are somewhat compromised by the partial nature of the examples chosen for discussion. Richard Ellman, *Romantic Codgers: Biographical Speculations*, Oxford, 1973, is a witty – sometimes whimsical – collection of studies of the relationship between biography and specific works of literature in the later Victorian and Edwardian period. Leslie Stephen, *Studies of a Biographer*, 4 vols., London, 1898–1902, a collection of essays by the first editor of the *Dictionary of National Biography*, is in itself a testimony to the increasing seriousness with which the form was then being taken, while its opening essay is a precursor of the many twentieth-century contributions by writers with practical experience of the form, not the least of whom is Stephen's daughter,

Virginia Woolf, whose two essays, 'The Art of Biography' and 'The New Biography' are reprinted in *Collected Essays*, ed., L. Woolf, vol. iv, London, 1967, along with various other biographical pieces. For accounts of biography as such in the twentieth century Garraty and Altick remain as the most substantial sources, but this century has seen a number of professional reflections, notably André Maurois, *Aspects of Biography*, New York, 1929, again a work revealing the influence of Bloomsbury, Leon Edel, *Literary Biography*, London 1957, which concerns itself particularly with the inter-relationship of biography and literary criticism, and J. L. Clifford, *From Puzzles to Portraits*, London, 1970, a lively account of the practise of biographical research and the application of its findings.

Index

A number of famous biographies are listed under their familiar rather than their full titles. In each case the familiar title is followed by the name of the author in brackets, e.g. *Life of Johnson* (Boswell).